COLIN BAXTER ISLAND GUIDES

Iona

E. Mairi MacArthur

Colin Baxter Photography, Grantown-on-Spey, Scotland

Sea road to Iona, from the south, plied by generations of pilgrims and settlers.
White horses race the Sound while a shaft of sun glints through squally clouds onto
the Abbey buildings and surrounding farmland.

Iona

Acknowledgements
The author is indebted to a number of people who have
contributed towards this book. Fiona Menzies provided the information for the geology
text and map while Jean Millar was likewise generous with text and list for the plants section.
Christine Clephan gave particularly helpful advice on the bird list and useful comments came too from
Richard Evans, Mark Jardine and Gordon Menzies. Local knowledge gleaned over the years,
from Dugald MacArthur, Oban, and from other natives of Iona, has again proved a
rich and much appreciated source. Responsibility for any errors or omissions,
however, rests with the author.

Archive photographs on pages 18, 19 and 22 courtesy of D. MacArthur.

First published in Great Britain in 1997 by
Colin Baxter Photography Ltd
Grantown-on-Spey,
Moray PH26 3NA
Scotland

Text © E. Mairi MacArthur 1997
Drawings © Iain Sarjeant 1997
Colour photographs © Colin Baxter 1997
Maps © Wendy Price 1997
Maps based on 1927 Ordnance Survey mapping, and on photography from
the Royal Commission on the Ancient and Historic Monuments of Scotland.

ISBN 1-900455-11-0

Front Cover Photograph IONA ABBEY, FROM THE WEST
Back Cover Photograph IONA FROM THE AIR, LOOKING SOUTH

Printed in Hong Kong

Contents

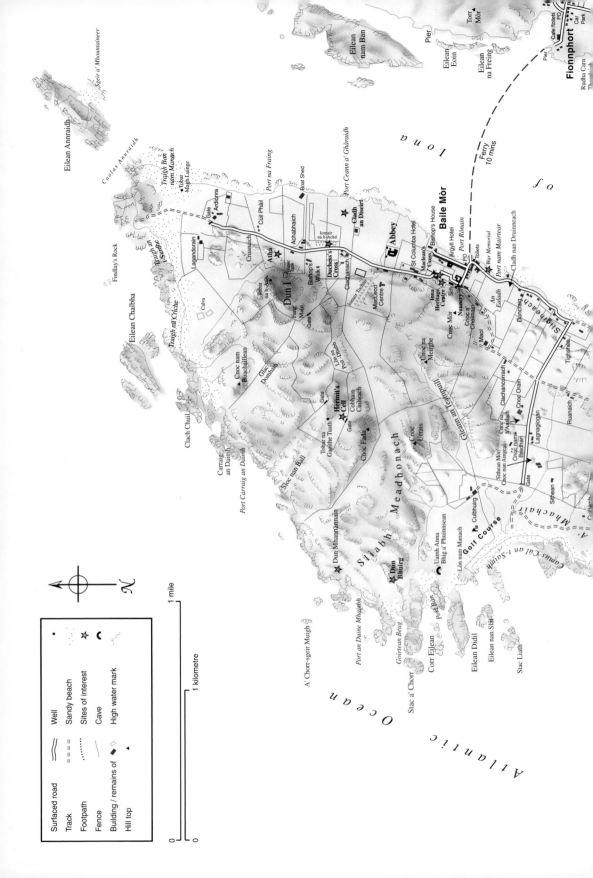

Boats Over Brine

Islands are by definition places set apart. To reach them, or return to them, we must venture over water. A seventh-century Irish poem celebrates a monk named Colum Cille as 'a sage across seas'. Along with a few companions, this voyager – to become revered in the Christian world as St Columba – was blown 'in boats over brine' towards the island we now call Iona.

A long time later, a man remembered simply as Seamus MacPhàraig (James son of Peter) composed a song of exile: *Nan robh mise mar bu chòir dhomh, thiginn air tìr an I Port Rònain* – 'if things were only as they ought I would be landing at Port Rònain on Iona'. Some time in the nineteenth century he had emigrated to the West Indies where, *fada thall air cùl na grèine* – 'far beyond the setting sun', he dreamed still of setting a course for the shores of home.

From the earliest times of human movement up and down our west coast, people have come and gone from this small island. A few have become indelibly associated with it and have contributed to its fame. Some have put down roots here, for longer or shorter periods. Most have left nothing but tantalising glimpses of their existence: materials unearthed by the plough or the archaeologist's trowel; rigs and furrows, long since grassed over; names among the hills; stones sunk in the turf.

This book will take you in the footsteps of many who have lived, worked and worshipped here over the centuries. We will try to read something of their story from clues left in the landscape, the buildings and the people's memories. Those who already know the island may follow well-trodden routes with us in their mind's eye and, perhaps, discover fresh aspects in familiar sights. For the newcomer, these detective trails will hopefully

A gem in the ocean. Grassland and heath, shell sand and rock, sea and skerry – the palette of fresh spring colour captured in this aerial photograph highlights the good natural resources that have long made Iona an attractive place to live.

9

provide an informative introduction and may whet the appetite. The bibliography points to the substantial body of published material which deals in more detail than is possible here with the archaeology, the architecture, the religious, social and natural history of the island.

And a Gaelic saying affirms that whoever goes to Iona will go not just once, but three times: *Am fear a thèid a dh'I, thèid e trì uairean ann.*

Today a broad, modern slipway at Port Rònain welcomes locals and visitors alike. Unless you have come by private yacht, or with one of the cruise ships which occasionally call, you will have made the briny crossing from Fionnphort, just over a kilometre (one mile) away on the neighbouring island of Mull. A ferry – but one which carries residents' cars only, plus those with a special permit – operates the short, regular service. Earlier, from the west coast port of Oban, you will have left the Scottish mainland on a larger passenger and vehicle ferry for the 40-minute sail to Craignure on the eastern side of Mull.

The 59 kilometres (35 miles) through Mull, with a coach party, by local bus service or by car, may take up to an hour, for traffic can be heavy in the summer season and the road is single-track. The fit may cycle or, indeed, hike over what is a splendidly scenic route in fine weather.

John Keats was less fortunate in July 1818, describing his tramp across Mull as 'a most wretched walk'. Foot-weary though the poet was, however, the journey's end astounded him: 'Who would expect to find the ruins of a fine Cathedral church, of cloisters, colleges, monasteries and nunneries in so remote an island?'

The richness of Iona's historic sites still comes as a surprise to some who make the trek westward. Conditioned as we are nowadays to road travel, it is tempting to think of the Hebrides as isolated, cut off by the sea from the mainstream of political and cultural life. Yet this was not always so. To understand fully the story of Iona it is crucial to remember that for many centuries it lay not on any land's periphery but, in several different respects, at the centre. For, when boats were the principal mode of transport, west coast waters brought together rather than separated the various peoples of present-day Ireland and Scotland. Christianity was to become another powerfully unifying force among those same tribes and Iona lay at the heart of this dynamic new movement. A recent book, *Iona. The Earliest Poetry of a Celtic Monastery* has, for good reason, a chapter headed 'Iona as a Literary Centre'. This important collection of sixth- and seventh-century poems, from which come the lines quoted in the first paragraph, reaffirms the cultural pre-eminence of this small island well over a thousand years ago.

At that time, and for most of the period since, the language in daily use on Iona was Gaelic. It declined steadily in the course of this century, the last generation of native speakers being born in the 1920s. The vast majority of local place-names derive from Gaelic, many of them throwing light on how the land was used.

The meaning of 'Iona' itself, however, has been long debated and never conclusively resolved. Over the last couple of hundred years various imaginative, but implausible, explanations have been advanced. It is commonly accepted that the word itself has a more prosaic origin – the misreading in a manuscript of *Ioua insula*, 'the island of I or Io'. That element is very old and remains obscure. Later Norse influence on Gaelic brought in a similar word *I*, corresponding to 'island', and *I Chaluim Chille* – the place or island of Columba – was for centuries the name used locally and repeated in many travellers' accounts. The modern Gaelic is simply *I* or *Eilean Idhe*.

The letter 'E' from the Book of Kells, a work of extraordinary beauty. An illuminated manuscript of the four Gospels, it was very probably made on Iona in the 8th century.

Historical Background

Those whose frail crafts of skin and wicker first scraped onto Iona's sand fashioned tools from stone and flint. From Neolithic times through to the Iron Age, i.e. from approximately 4000 BC up to AD 400, the fertile raised beach along the island's east side was periodically cultivated. Deposits of bones and shells indicate that settlers also found the surrounding waters abundant in fish and shellfish. Dun Bhuirg on the west coast was occupied towards the end of that period. A kerbed burial-cairn at the eastern foot of Cnoc Mòr may date much further back, to the second millennium BC.

Excavations on Iona to date have focused largely on or around its ecclesiastical sites. In future, perhaps, the archaeologist's eye may decipher some more of its secular history and help clarify whether indeed the island was continuously inhabited during the centuries prior to Columba's arrival. It is very unlikely that he came to a deserted place, for here was good, relatively sheltered land at the centre of a strategic sea route. Iona lay on the rim of territories occupied by the northern Picts while, some time in the fifth century, settlers from the kingdom of Dál Riata in Ireland gained a foothold on what is now the south Argyll mainland. It may well have been Conall, king of this Scottish Dál Riata and a relative of Columba, who guided him towards Iona. The island was an attractive, practical spot in which to found a monastery.

The year, so far as can be ascertained, was AD 563 and Columba was about 42 years old. He had grown up in an age of rapidly expanding religious activity in Ireland, where the founders of new and inspirational communities

Replica of the eighth-century St John's Cross forms a mosaic in stone against the restored early Christian chapel, known as St Columba's Shrine. The materials may be modern but the resonance is age-old.

were soon endowed with sanctity by the next generation. By the time of his death, in AD 597, the cult of Columba was probably well established.

A century later, Adomnán, ninth abbot of Iona, brought together stories passed down within the family of monks, and his own vision of how such an illustrious predecessor should be portrayed, in his *Life of Columba*. This is not a biographical life-story in the sense we know today, but a series of incidents demonstrating the saint's prophetic and miraculous powers. Nevertheless, its pages reveal valuable details about daily life in sixth- and seventh-century Iona and confirm the monastery's highly influential status in its heyday.

Richard Sharpe, whose excellent new edition of the *Life* was published in 1995, points out that it is through Adomnán's words that we come closest to Columba; no surviving manuscripts can be attributed with certainty to the hand of the saint himself. But, he warns, the creation of a legend was a complex process. Through the eleventh and twelfth centuries particularly and up until our own times, ever more elaborate layers of myth and folklore attached themselves to the saint's deeds and sayings.

Only in medieval sources, for instance, do stories of forced exile or contrition after battle emerge as reasons for Columba's departure. Adomnán states simply that since boyhood this young Irish nobleman had trained for a life in holy orders and that he 'sailed away from Ireland to Britain, choosing to be a pilgrim for Christ'.

Whatever led up to its foundation, Iona was without doubt one of the great centres of the early church in these islands. Succeeding generations of monks kept strong personal and political links with Ireland and with Columban houses up and down the Scottish west coast. River mouths and sea lochs were open invitations to these bold and experienced sailors. And so missionaries from the strengthening network probed ever farther north and east into the lands of the Picts and, ultimately, south to Northumbria.

The island became a hive of art and learning.

Map from Bishop William Reeves' edition of Adomnán's *Life of Columba*, 1857. 'Hy' was an old form of Iona's name; the map also records a large number of Gaelic place-names plus the main agricultural divisions, including the two *sliabh* or moorland areas.

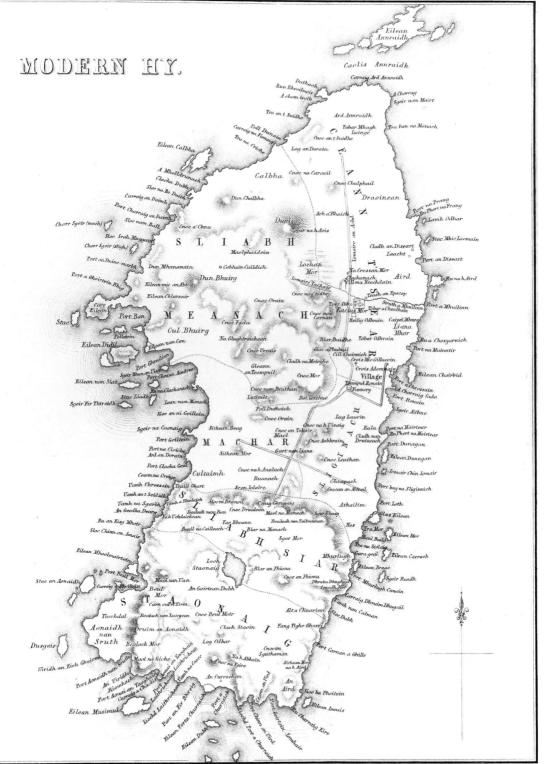

MODERN HY.

Eilean Annraidh

Caolis Annraidh

Carraig Ard Annraidh

Dathach
Rua Bheoilvair
A chan leoth
Tra an t Suidhe
Poll Dunain
Carraig na Fennig
Tra na Criche

A Charraig
Sgeir nam Mairt

Ard Annraidh

Tobar Mhagh
Lainge

Tra ban na Manach

Cnoc an t Suidhe

Lag an Dorain

Eilean Calbha

A Mhelldrunach
Clacha Dubh
Sloc na Bo Duibh
Carraig an Daimh
Port Charraig an Daimh
Sloc nam Ball

Calbha

Dun Chalbha

Cnoc na Carcail

Cnoc Chalphail

Port na Frang
Ru Phort na Frang

Draoinean

Ach a'Bhaich

Lamh Odhar
Stac Mhic Laomain

Chorr Sgeir (muich)
Chorr Sgeir (stigh)
Port an Duine marbh
Port a Ghoirtein Bhig

Dun Mhananain
Cobhain Cuildich

Maolphaidein

Cnoc a'Chnu

SLIABH

Dun
Tobar na h Avis

Cladh an Diseart
Leachd

Port an Diseart

Dun Bhuirg

Lochan
Mor

Na Cressan Mor
Clachanach

Aird

Run a h Aird

Eilean mic an Aba
Eilean Chlarsair

Iomaire Tachair

Cnoc nan eidhe

Allma Neachdain

Teach an Epscop

Port a Mhuilinn

Corr
Eilein

Cnoc Orain

Iomaire an Achd

Struth a Mhuilinn
Tobar a Cheathan

Stac
Port Ban
Pollerin

MEANACH

Cnoc Fada

Cnoc nan
Carnan

Eaclus Mor
Reilig Odhrain

Caipel Mhuire
Liana
Mhor

Eilean Didil
Eilean nan Con
Cul Bhuirg

Na Ghughtraichean

Tobar Odhrain

Rua Chosgarnich
Port na Muirutir

Sgeir Bhan an Uisd
Port Ghraliam
Port Cleann Aindra

Cnoc Urcais

Blar Buidhe

Glac a'Phuill

Cill Chainnich
Crois Mic Gillaevin

Eilean Chairbid

Eilean nan Slat
Run a Clachanach
Stac Liadh

Gleann
an Teampuil

Cladh na Meirghe

Crois Adomnain

Sgeir Fir Thdreidh
Loan nam Manach

Cnoc Mor

Village

Port a Chrossain
A Charraig fada

Sgeir na Caonaig
Sloc an ni Goillein

Cnoc nam Bruthan
Lathuil

Teampul Ronain
Sionney

Port Ronain
Sgeir Aithne

Poll Duthaich
Bol Leithne

Sitheam Beag

Cnoc Orain

Lag Laurin

Eala
Cladh nan
Druincach

Port na Mairtear
Ru Phort na Mairtear

MACHAR

Cnoc an Tobair
Cnoc Aobhrain

Cnoc na h Uneig

Port Dunagan

Port Greittein
Port na Cloiche
Ard an Dorain

Sitheam Mor

Gart nan Liana

Cnoc Leathan

Eilean Dunagan

Port Clacha Geal
Ceann na Creige

Cnoc nah Analach
Ruanach

SLIGINACH

Iomair Chin Iomair
Port beg na Sliginich

Vamh Chrossain
Vamh an t Seidlar

Traill Ghart

Scot Iolaire

Cheapach
Gnocan an Biteal

Port Loth

Vamh na Sgarbh
An Geodha Dearg

Vamh a Bhodaich
Sloc na Bhodaich

Slocra Branril
Cnoc Druidean

Craig Chruagig
Maol na Manach

Athailim

Glas Eilean

Ru an Eisg Mhuir
Sloc Chinn an Amuir

Nah Uchdaichean

Ear Bheann
Buail na Cailleach

Bealach nan Tuibhnean
Blar na Manach

Sgur Bhoin
Nos

Tra Mor
Beal Buaig
Tra na Siolag

Eilean Mor

Eilean Mhaolmuirteln

SLIABH SIAR

Sgur Mor

Mharlugh

Cara geal

Eilean Carrach

Stac an Aonaidh
Port Beul Mor
Carraig a Mhullain

Beul
Mor

Maol nan Van

Loch
Staonaig

Blar an Fhiona

Cnoc an Fhiona
Dhraim Dhugail
Iomath Mor

Eilean Breac
Port Mharlugh Canuin

Sgeir Ruadh

Tiochdal
Bealach nan Luirgean

An Goirtean Dubh
Cnoc Beul Moir

Carn cul t Eirin

STAONAIG

Carraig Dhruim Dhugail
Cnoc nan Calman

Aonaidh
nan
Sruth

Dusgeir

Druim an Aonaidh
Bealach Mor

Clach Staoin

Lag Odhar

Alt a Chaoriov

Fang Tighe Ghorr
Sloc Dubh

Port Carnan a Grille

Viridh an Eich Ghuirm

Maol na Giche

Na h Abhain
Cnoc na Faire

Cnocan
Sguthaman

Sitheam Mor
na h Aird

An Uiridh
An Riomhach
Port Aonai an Taoghain
Carraig a Chaolis

Aonai an Taoghain
Leabha Leithrichean

An Currachan

Iomath an Tind

An
Aird

Sloc ba Fheitein

Eilean Musimul

Liachd Leithrichean
Port an Fir Bheoil
Eilean Porta Churraich

Camh na Casc
Port a
Churraich

Doire Bhein an Tiod

Port Goirtein Iomhair

Sloc Charraig Eire

Eilean Iuvais

Eilean Dubh

Rua a Churraich

Engd. by J. Bartholomew Junr. Edinburgh

Chronicles of events were listed, thus bequeathing – through later copies – an invaluable record for historians. Prayers and poems were composed. Psalms and scripture were illuminated with marvellous skill and creativity. The earliest of the magnificent high crosses were carved in the mid eighth century. Only three of these survive and there may have been others dating from even earlier.

But brutal change was on the way. Between 795 and 806 Viking raiders ransacked and burned the buildings and slew 68 monks. Abbot Cellach of Iona founded a new Columban house at Kells in Ireland, probably transferring there for safety the island's library and the famed gospel now known as the Book of Kells. Although depleted, Iona was never deserted and close links were kept between the two communities. Cellach's successor Diarmait was styled Abbot of Iona and in 825 the venerated shrine of Columba was still there, hidden successfully from another attack that year.

In 849, however, the saint's relics were divided

The prominent Dun Bhuirg near the west coast made an obvious, easily defended hill fort for the islanders around the turn of the first millennium.

between Kells and Dunkeld. This was, perhaps, to underscore that the centre of political gravity had by now swung east with the seizing of Pictland by Kenneth MacAlpin. Abbots of Iona continue to appear in the Irish annals until the early eleventh century but the monastery's influence was much diminished.

Religious life on Iona was reinvigorated early in the thirteenth century with the establishment of a Benedictine Monastery and, shortly afterwards, a Nunnery. It is these buildings which form the major part of the historic sites on Iona today. The new Abbey's first benefactor belonged to a family very much in the ascendancy in West Highland politics at that period, the MacDonalds. Reginald was the son of Somerled, founder of a powerful Gaelic-Norse dynasty known as the Lords of the Isles. Scholarship, art and an Iona school of sculpture flourished once more. Chieftains and other members of Gaeldom's leading families were brought for burial in the island's sacred soil.

From 1499 Iona was also the seat of the Bishop of the Isles, reflecting its continuing prestige, and the abbey church acted as Cathedral of the Isles. But the monastic community began to dwindle. As the sixteenth century advanced, so also did the influence in Argyll and the southern isles of the Campbell family who were protestant sympathisers. This probably helped ensure that the Reformation, when it came, passed peaceably on Iona. There is no evidence of undue destruction and the few remaining monks and nuns appear to have lived on, unmolested, until they left or died. The Macleans of Duart had gradually acquired most of the former Abbey and Nunnery lands but by 1691 their financial and political position had weakened; they were unable to resist the seizure of their possessions, including Iona, by the Earl of Argyll who landed a regiment on Mull that year.

The fabric of the now empty buildings on Iona fell prey to the elements and to the quarrying instincts of locals eager for building materials. The Governor of the Isle of Man, Dr Sacheverell, who visited in 1688, and naturalist and minister Dr John Walker, there in 1764, both reported that the islanders, although miserably poor and without the services of a parish minister, remained devout and gathered within the crumbling walls of the cathedral on Sundays for private prayer.

From about this time the local inhabitants become much more visible in the pages of documented history. They were frequently mentioned by travellers, whose numbers surged as antiquarian interest blossomed towards the end of the eighteenth century. James Boswell, in 1773, was impressed by the islanders' virtual self-sufficiency, including the brewing of beer, and by the simple fare he and Dr Johnson were offered: cuddies (coalfish) and some oysters boiled in butter, potatoes and a mug of milk.

An anonymous diarist in 1788 relates more details of the local economy. The people bred cattle and horses for sale, exported barley and earned extra cash from kelp gathering. They fetched peat from Mull for their fires and burned fish- or seal-oil in their lamps. He found the people longlived and prolific, and a schoolmaster

Gathering of Church of Scotland clergymen and dignitaries on 9 June 1897 outside the abbey west door. Four services, two each in Gaelic and English, were held under a temporary roof to mark the 1300th anniversary of St Columba's death.

teaching Gaelic, English, writing and the five rules of arithmetic to 25 pupils.

From the time a secular community sprang up alongside the monastic one – possibly during the Columban era and certainly by the medieval period – its main settlement was a rough cluster of low stone huts above Port Rònain, straggling towards the west side of the Abbey boundary. An estate map drawn by William Douglas in 1769 confirms this. Under the system known as 'runrig', the rent-paying tenants worked a given number of arable strips, rotating these annually by lot. Agricultural reform begun by the fifth Duke of Argyll in the late eighteenth century, however, radically altered this pattern and resulted in the landscape which we see today. He called first for a census and found that, in 1779, the island supported 249 inhabitants. Around 1802 he ordered its division into 30 individual holdings, or crofts, and the farming tenantry gradually moved out to build homes on the fields they had been allocated. The

Abbey ruins in the late 19th century, captured on film by George Washington Wilson from a corner of the overgrown graveyard.

village was rebuilt to form a trim street facing the sea.

The population rose steadily, family incomes often supplemented by earnings from the young men and women at seasonal harvest or labouring work in the lowlands. The highest recorded figure totalled 521 in 1835. But for this large number to survive principally from the fruits of land and sea left the people increasingly vulnerable to bad harvests or fluctuations in stock prices. In 1846 disaster struck. Up and down the west Highlands blight devastated the potato crop. In Iona it was called 'A' bhliadhna a dh' fhalbh am buntàta', 'the year the potato went away'.

Virtually overnight the people lost a staple food, for themselves and for the beasts they sold to pay the rent. Relief measures helped prevent outright famine but sickness, debt and hardship endured for nearly a decade as the potatoes continued to fail. By the mid-1850s about a third of the entire population had taken up the Argyll Estate's offer of assistance with fares and sailed for Canada or Australia.

Vacated crofts were amalgamated to make bigger units and to this day these form the three farms of Culbhuirg, Maol and St Columba. Eighteen crofts remained. Crops and cattle prices revived and, after the Crofters' Act of 1886 brought security of tenure and the lowering of contested rents, a degree of stability returned to the local economy. This received a small annual boost, too, from the growing number of visitors who rented cottages in summer or stayed at the two hotels. The steamship era had boomed since its early days in the 1820s. Each summer crowds flocked on board at Oban for the day trip to Staffa and Iona, sealed with royal approval after the cruise in 1847 by Queen Victoria and Prince Albert. Towards the close of the century, in June 1897, the islanders were joined by hundreds of visitors for services commemorating the 1300th anniversary of the death of St Columba.

At the first census of the twentieth century, in 1901, Iona's population was 213 and as the last decade opened in 1991, it stood at 130. A much bigger proportion of these residents are incomers but several families can trace their roots back to the core of tenants who worked the

A corner of the old Post Office on the village brae, a busy hub of island life from 1896 until 1988.

land and sea here 200 years ago and more. Nowadays a living is provided by agriculture and a small amount of fishing, along with tourist-related services and crafts.

The twentieth century also brought great changes. In 1899 the eighth Duke of Argyll gifted the ecclesiastical buildings to a newly formed public trust linked to the Church of Scotland. It was his express wish 'that the Cathedral shall be re-roofed and restored' and he hoped, too, that all denominations be permitted to worship there. Between 1902 and 1905, and again in 1909-10, the Iona Cathedral Trustees raised funds for and oversaw the rebuilding of the Abbey choir and nave. After a celebratory inaugural service on 26 June 1910 the church was used regularly for local worship.

Between 1938 and 1965 the adjoining cloisters and monastic buildings were restored by the Iona Community, founded by the Revd George F. MacLeod for that purpose. Ministering to an urban parish during the Depression years had convinced him of the growing gap between the Church and the real concerns of daily life. This quest for spiritual renewal was to be rooted in a task of physical renewal, as young ministers worked alongside joiners and stonemasons to raise again the walls of the medieval Monastery.

It was a vision pursued with single-minded energy although not without controversy. Concerns about its radical nature were expressed in the wider arena of the Church of Scotland and on the island itself, where the parish minister and elders had no involvement in the project. Lord MacLeod of Fuinary, formerly the Revd George MacLeod, granted a life peerage in 1967, died in 1991 at the age of 96.

In 1979, nearly three centuries of continuous ownership by the Earls and later the Dukes of Argyll came to an end when Iona was put up for sale by the Trustees of the Argyll Estates. For the twelfth Duke, breaking such a link was a matter for deep regret but one made necessary by an unavoidable burden of death duties. The island was bought for the nation by the Hugh Fraser

Angus MacKay, on the ladder, thatching Highland Cottage in the village in the 1920s. Helping him are Archibald MacArthur, Charlie Kirkpatrick and Duncan MacGillivray. A communal task, the new roof of straw or bent grass would be in place within the day.

Foundation and, after a few months under the direct administration of the Secretary of State for Scotland, it passed into the care of the National Trust for Scotland (NTS). This change did not affect the Iona Cathedral Trust which retained sole responsibility for the Abbey and Nunnery buildings and the graveyard.

Iona is not merely a collection of historic sites. It is a living and working island, home to a permanent local community. Visitors are welcome but should remember that they must share the roads and facilities with people going about their daily business, and the landscape with those whose livelihoods depend in part upon it.

Mindful of the need to reconcile these twin pressures, the National Trust for Scotland's five-year management plan for the island includes detailed consideration of such items as access, impact on sensitive areas, site interpretation and the care of those archaeological remains in their charge. The plan, which leads up to the year 2000, has been prepared in consultation with the island's Community Council, the Iona Cathedral Trust and the Iona Community.

Still in progress at the time of writing are a proposal for a visitor orientation point near the pier and attempts to identify land suitable for informal camping on a limited scale. There has never been a formal campsite on the island and camping at random is not permitted. Also underway is a survey of the most regularly used tracks in the hill areas, with a view to discreet footpath maintenance.

Meanwhile, common sense observation of the countryside code by visitors will be much appreciated by the crofters and farmers. Fences should not be climbed; if no gate or stile is evident it is best to avoid the area. Fasten gates securely. Do not cross fields containing crops or livestock and be particularly careful not to disturb ewes and lambs in spring. Dogs should be kept under control at all times and on the leash anywhere where there may be livestock; it may be better not to bring them at all in the lambing season. Please do not leave litter and do respect the general peace and quiet of the island.

The Landscape

'This Ile…full of little hillocks, pleasant and healthfull with a store of common medicinall herbs… The Ile is fruitfull and has plaine arable ground in good measure, interlyned betwixt the little green hills…'

These words come from a manuscript description of Iona written in 1693 by Sir Robert Sibbald and their sentiment was echoed many times by later visitors to the island. First impressions of Iona are indeed of a fertile landscape, low-lying though not flat, and very green. The usual approach is from the north or east where fields and grassy meadows border almost two-thirds of the coastline. Another broad band of arable stretches across the middle to meet the sandy turf of the western machair land.

The rougher hilly areas, in the north-west corner and the southern third of the island, are quite different in character. Here the greys and browns of rock and moorland seem at first glance to predominate, although in fact there are many pockets of vivid green sheltered by steep gullies or at the head of small bays. There is plenty of colour too in the rich variety of flowers, underfoot or clinging to cliffs, and in the late summer's carpet of purple heather.

Iona is about 5.5 km (3 miles) in length, 1.5 km (1 mile) across at its narrowest, and has a total area of just under 800 ha (2000 acres). The highest hill, Dun I, is only 101 metres (332 ft) above sea-level. Here are no soaring peaks, yet there is something about this landscape, on its diminutive scale, that is pleasingly deceptive. The rugged hillocks and craggy ravines can seem to tower around the lone walker, enclosing him or her in a miniature mountain range.

There is not a particularly long list of wildlife native to Iona. Otters are occasionally found among rocks and in streams above the shoreline, whereas seals breed only on some of the off-lying islets. Weasels and stoats were once

Looking south from the rugged pasture of the northern hill ground towards the smooth green stretch of the Machair.

quite common. Mice and rats still frequent farm buildings, inevitably, and rabbits burrow into the machair land although they are not as numerous as before. According to visitor H.D. Graham, the man who had first introduced them to the island was still alive in 1850.

Heath Spotted-orchid, found frequently in the marshy moorland areas of the island.

A more recent and very unwelcome invasion has been that of escaped mink, which play havoc with breeding colonies of tern and other seabirds and with local poultry. The islanders are trying their best to eradicate this predatory species.

Iona is classed as a Regional Scenic Area by the local authority and also forms part of the Argyll Islands Environmentally Sensitive Area (ESA). Under the ESA scheme, islanders can be compensated for adopting certain measures to maximise conservation. These designations recognise the outstanding quality of Iona's landscape and the potential it has to sustain areas of ecological and historic value.

GEOLOGY

Iona's western half is made of rocks called Lewisian Gneiss, so named because they are similar to those on the island of Lewis. At about 2800 million years old, these rocks are among the oldest on Earth, although there are many rocks older than 3000 million years in places such as Greenland and Australia. The age of the Earth is thought to be 4600 million years.

The rocks of western Iona are made from many varieties of early sedimentary and igneous rock which have been transformed to banded gneisses by the high pressures and temperatures deep in the Earth's crust. Gneisses are a type of metamorphic rock (from the Greek *meta*, 'change' and *morphic*, 'form'). After the gneisses were formed they gradually rose from the depths of the Earth's crust up to the surface.

About 1000 million years ago, the west coast of Scotland

was a low-lying landscape composed of the gneisses described above. To the north-west were huge mountains, as big as the Himalayas, with no vegetation – none existed by this date – so that erosion happened very fast. The sediments from this erosion were deposited on the Lewisian gneisses and, in due course, became the rocks now found from the north coast to just north of the Marble Quarry. The first sediments to be deposited were boulders, then came small pebbles, then sands and muds. All these sediments sank under the weight of those above and gradually hardened into rocks. (You can see this sequence of rocks across the north end.) All this happened before there was a single hard-shelled creature on Earth. The first hard-shelled fossils date from about 600 million years ago. Thus, no fossils are to be found on Iona.

Approximately 400 million years ago, the whole of eastern Scotland was pushed over western Scotland along a thrust plane stretching from Durness down past the east side of Iona. Along this plane the rocks became highly crushed and unrecognisable. Soon after the thrusting, hot, molten granite rose into the area of the thrust plane to form the large body of pink granite lying between Fionnphort and Bunessan on Mull. The granite can be seen close to Iona, on the little islets off Traighmòr beach.

About 60 million years ago, some time after the American and European continents had started drifting

Large erratic boulder of pink granite, cast up on the eastern shoreline of Iona.

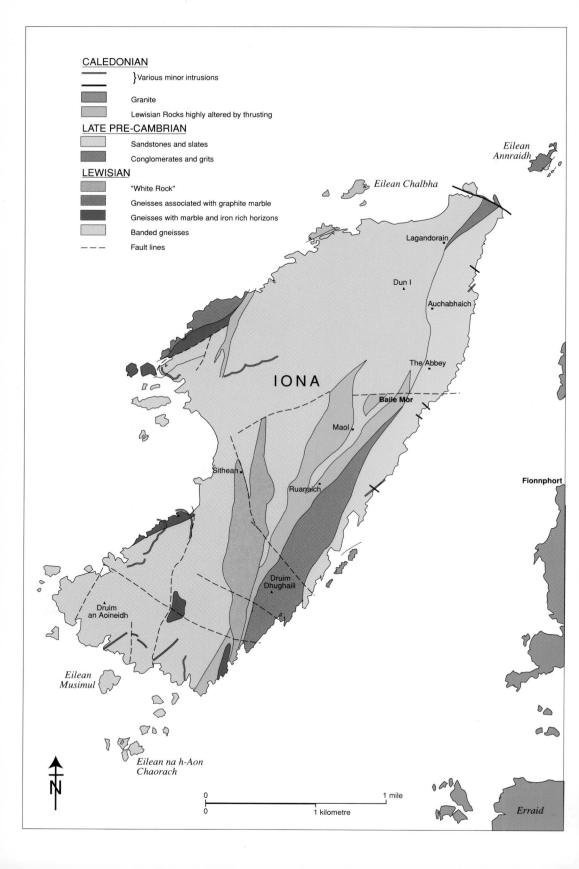

CALEDONIAN

⎫
⎬ Various minor intrusions
⎭

Granite

Lewisian Rocks highly altered by thrusting

LATE PRE-CAMBRIAN

Sandstones and slates

Conglomerates and grits

LEWISIAN

"White Rock"

Gneisses associated with graphite marble

Gneisses with marble and iron rich horizons

Banded gneisses

- - - Fault lines

Eilean Annraidh

Eilean Chalbha

Lagandorain

Dun I ▲

Auchabhaich ■

The Abbey

Baile Mòr ■

I O N A

Maol ■

Sithean ■

Ruanaich ■

Fionnphort

Druim Dhughaill ▲

Druim an Aoineidh ▲

Eilean Musimul

Eilean na h-Aon Chaorach

N

0   1 mile
0   1 kilometre

Erraid

apart, there was a period of great volcanic activity in the region. A succession of three volcanoes, centred behind Ben More, spewed out vast quantities of lava over the whole area. Staffa and the Treshnish Islands are remnants of these lava flows; the columns of Staffa formed while the lava cooled. The lava flows that used to cover Iona and the Ross of Mull have since been completely eroded away.

During the ice ages Mull and Iona were covered by a thick sheet of ice, maybe 1.6 km (1 mile) deep. This ice sheet moved westwards over Mull and Iona, grinding smooth all the rocks in its path. The weight of the ice pushed the land downwards and when it melted, the land slowly rose up again. Three levels of raised beaches can be seen on Iona: the highest level is visible behind the Iona Pottery, just north of the abbey; the abbey itself sits on the mid-level beach; and the village is on the lowest level. Evidence of the westward movement of the ice is clear from the large variety of pebbles on Iona's beaches, some from as far afield as Oban.

BIRDS

Iona may not boast the major ornithological interest of some larger islands, such as Islay, or the nesting stacks of, say, St Kilda, but its varied habitats shelter a broad range of birds nonetheless.

There have been changes, inevitably, over the centuries. One informative and entertaining historical source is *The Birds of Iona*, compiled from letters written by Henry D. Graham between 1851 and c.1871. Graham lived on Iona, as guest of the Free Church minister, between 1848 and 1854 and on the Argyll mainland thereafter.

As was the custom of the times, one of Graham's main objectives was to shoot his feathered friends, either for the pot or to be despatched cheerfully for stuffing. But his words and sketches provide a fascinating window onto the birdlife of the island and its surrounding waters more than a century ago.

One January he chanced on rare visitors: 'numerous flocks of snow bunting cowering among the stubble, the

Geological map of Iona showing the main rock types.

29

males in beautiful white plumage'. Arctic terns were so
plentiful, on the other hand, that their eggs were
eaten and cormorant soup, which tasted very like
hare, was recommended. The note of the stone
chat reminded Graham of a geologist chipping
away and he was much taken with the
brilliant coral bill and glossy black plumage
of the chough, said by the natives to be
'St Columba's bird'. These birds had long
bred in the Abbey ruins and their decline,
and eventual disappearance, was thought to
stem from increased disturbance by visitors.

Corncrake, seldom seen
but still heard near a few
of Iona's arable fields in
summer.

On 12 May 1852 Graham wrote that
corncrakes had arrived: 'Their appearance is so precisely
punctual to the day that I would as soon date by it as I
would by the almanac'. All the meadows and cornfields
then rang with the male's 'monotonous' cry, and, he hinted
darkly, they made 'very good eating'. Today, in contrast, the
corncrake is internationally endangered and parts of the
Hebrides provide its last refuge in Britain. Several crofters
and farmers on Iona take part in the Royal Society for the
Protection of Birds (RSPB) / Scottish Natural Heritage (SNH)
management scheme to protect the four or five pairs which
return each year. This can involve keeping tall vegetation
such as iris or reeds, the birds' preferred cover, and cutting
hay later rather than earlier, to allow the chicks to hatch.

The cuckoo still calls in spring, from the trees behind
the Manse, and other bird cries remain very familiar – gull
and oyster-catcher, curlew and skylark to name but a few. It
would be good if the elusive corncrake, rarely seen,
manages to survive on Iona and continues to add its
curious, grating song to the early summer chorus.

PLANTS

Compared with Mull, Iona is considerably more fertile and,
although there is much overlap with its larger neighbour,
the island supports a distinctive range of flower and plant
life. The soil along the east side and in the strip across the
centre owes its fertility to the deposits of calcareous sand

and to the comparative shelter from the prevailing westerly winds. Traditional farming methods, with little herbicide or imported fertiliser, mean that some arable weeds now rare on the mainland still flourish here. The machair land on the north and west shores supports a specialist flora of dwarfed plants, which have adapted to survive heavy grazing and exposure to strong, salt-laden winds.

On the sandy seashore, the plants must contend with even more extreme conditions of salt air and lack of fresh water. Marram grass holds the shifting sands and builds up dunes that provide some shelter for other plants. In recent years an NTS programme to stabilise the dunes of the north end, by seeding them with marram, has been underway.

The parts of the island which are neither inhabited nor arable are known in Gaelic as *an sliabh* which means a tract of moorland and each is referred to locally as 'the hill'. The soil here is acidic with heath plants growing on the drier parts, while in the wetter areas typical bog plants are found. There are many steep gullies and rock faces in this area which escape the grazing by sheep and cattle and are rich with flowers and dwarfed trees. On some especially favoured ledges blown sand has mixed with the peaty soil, making them ideal sites for some of the most attractive and unusual flowers of the island. Fortunately for the history of plant recording on Iona, visitors over the centuries have included several with expert knowledge of botany. The Revd John Lightfoot accompanied Thomas Pennant in 1772; William Hooker was a nineteenth century botanist who visited Iona; William Keddie and George Ross did likewise, both producing plant lists.

Comprehensive fieldwork carried out from 1966-70 by the Department of Botany, British Museum (Natural History) covered Mull and Iona and the results were published in 1978. Jean M. Millar has maintained a close interest in Iona's botany; her first list of 200 species, published in 1972, had more than doubled for a second edition in 1993. The NTS has undertaken a full ecological survey and keeps a watching brief on changes which may affect the vegetation of the island.

The Gaelic for Slender St John's Wort is *Lus Chaluim Chille* (Columba's flower), and it was long used in herbal ointments. Tradition claims that the Saint cured an overwrought herdboy by placing a poultice of the plant in his armpit.

The Village – Am Baile Mòr

In the summer of 1893 a visitor named Malcolm Ferguson leaned on the rail of the steamship *Grenadier*, while his fellow-passengers were rowed ashore in sturdy red tenders, and relished 'a splendid bird's-eye view...the village, with all the sacred, ancient and historic edifices of the place nestled pretty close together...along the face of a sunny, gently sloping hillside'.

Iona's main secular settlement has always been situated close to its religious sites. It was, and is, impossible for the visitor to experience one without the other. The Gaelic name for the village, **Baile Mòr**, means 'big township' and although it hardly seems large to a modern city-dweller, the term simply indicates that here was the place where most of the population lived.

The island lacks a natural harbour, in particular one with shelter from the fierce southerly gales. In the days of sail various creeks and beaches along the eastern shore were at times used, if wind and tide dictated. But the main landing-place has long been **Port Rònain**, below the village. Here Dr Samuel Johnson was carried ashore, dry-shod, in 1773 and was at once moved to utter words which have probably been the most often quoted among the thousands ever written about Iona:

A familiar red sign gleams cheerfully at the head of the sandy bay right by the landing-place. Visitors heading up from the ferry, seen approaching in the background, make the wee whitewashed Post Office a regular port of call.

> We were now treading that illustrious island, which was once the luminary of the Caledonian regions, whence savage clans and roving barbarians derived the benefits of knowledge and the blessings of religion. ...That man is little to be envied whose patriotism would not gain force upon the plain of Marathon, or whose piety would not grow warmer among the ruins of Iona.

Village Plan

Cnoc Mòr

Burial Cairn

Torr Gorm

Surgery

Manse and Heritage Centre

Parish Church

Seat

Gate

Village Hall

Library

School

Sraid nam Marbh

MacLean's Cross

Gate

Darrach Beag

Nunnery

Gate

Fraser Memorial Cairn

Stile

Pairc nan Croisean

Iona Scottish Crafts

Teampull Rònain

Gàradh Marsaili

Phones

Shop

Footpath

Argyll Hotel

Block House
Roseneath
White Ho
Primrose Cot
Lovedale Cot
Tigh na Traigh

Knocknacross
Mo Dhachaidh
Highland Cot
Shuna
Ballymore
Oran Cot
Victoria Cot
Staffa Cot
Tigh na Beairt
Arnish Ho

Iona Cottage

St Ronan's

General Store

Seaview

Duart

Dunara

Post Office

Lorne Cottage

Toilets

Carraig Fhada

Martyrs Bay Restaurant

St Ronan's Bay

Pier

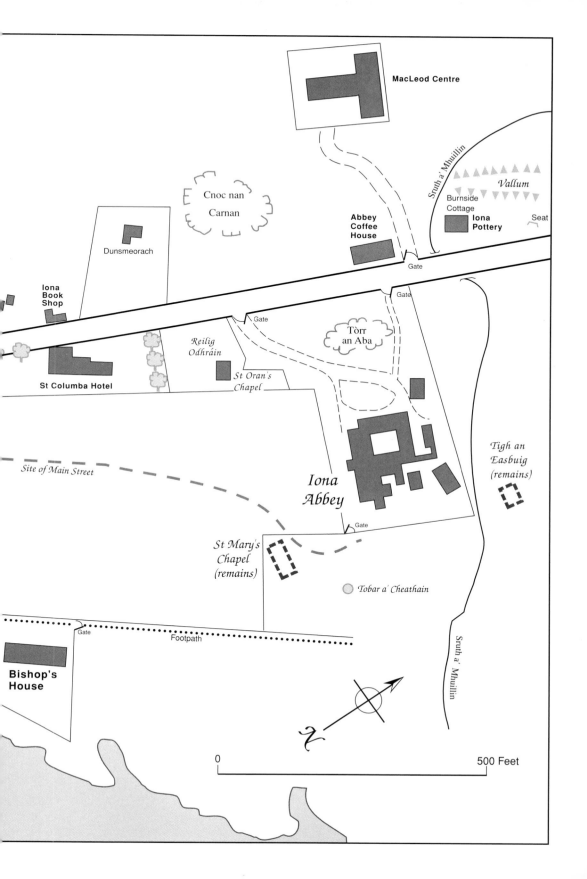

MacLeod Centre

Sruth a' Mhuillin

Cnoc nan
Carnan

Vallum

Burnside
Cottage

Abbey
Coffee
House

Iona
Pottery

Seat

Dunsmeorach

Gate

Gate

Iona
Book
Shop

Gate

Tòrr
an Aba

*Reilig
Odhráin*

St Columba Hotel

*St Oran's
Chapel*

Iona
Abbey

*Tigh an
Easbuig
(remains)*

Site of Main Street

Gate

*St Mary's
Chapel
(remains)*

Tobar a' Cheathain

Gate

Footpath

Sruth a' Mhuillin

Bishop's
House

0

500 Feet

A natural outcrop at Port Rònain, the Carraig Fhada (long rock), served the islanders for many years as a rough landing-quay. At low tide iron rings for mooring ropes may still be seen embedded in it. A journal from 1837 records one boatload's hazardous arrival, as passengers slithered over seaweed, plonked into pools and one or two over-confident unfortunates 'rolled over on their backs and got a sound ducking'.

The first jetty was built in 1850 as part of a programme of public works during the potato famine years. Improvements were made at intervals over the next century until, in 1979, a substantially larger slipway was begun for the new car-ferry service. This was broadened in 1994 to accommodate the most recent, larger vessel.

Just above the sands of Port Rònain, and first on the right as you turn into the village street, is a low white building where the **Post Office** is currently housed. In the 1920s and 1930s this was the store for a shop and tea-room opposite, run by Martha MacLeod. For centuries news reached the island by messenger or word of mouth but in 1851 Archibald MacDonald was appointed its first postmaster. Two generations of MacDonalds operated the Post Office from a small single-storey building near the south end of the street, known as the White House.

In 1896 another local family began a long association with postal services, when Angus MacPhail took over. The following year he built a new Post Office and shop on the brae which leads immediately up from the jetty, installing a telegraph service in time to send Queen Victoria a message of goodwill from the islanders for the Diamond Jubilee of her reign that year. Gathering in this small corrugated iron edifice, painted blue, to wait for the evening mail, exchange news, buy a leg of mutton or a Goss china souvenir, remains a vivid holiday memory for many.

In 1990 the building was replaced by a general store, open all year. Between it and a craft shop, open during the tourist season, are the island's two public telephone boxes and a local noticeboard.

In the foreground, a broad flagstone step leads into the chapter-house of the medieval Nunnery. Beyond is a corner of the cloister garth, where the sisters walked and tended herbs. A gull perches above the Romanesque windows of their small church.

On the opposite side of the road there once lay a flat granite stone, slightly hollowed in the centre. This was the **Clach a' Bhainne** (milk-stone). Girls returning with milk from cows out on the pastures would pour a drop onto the stone as an offering to the gruagach, a spirit said to look after the cattle. How long this superstitious custom was observed is impossible to say, but Iona was one of many Highland places where folklorist Alexander Carmichael saw a milk-stone late last century. Knowledge of its location, now some way beneath the tarmac, lingered on until well within living memory.

Remnants of pagan belief lie cheek by jowl with signs of Christian witness in a place so small as Iona.

Just steps from where the cattle's fairy guardian was appeased, you turn into the Nunnery, the quiet grassy precincts where devout Augustinian nuns once lived. Locally it was called *An Eaglais Dhubh*, literally 'the black church' as the Gaelic word for nun is *cailleach-dhubh*, meaning 'the veiled and black-robed one'. The ruins

37

themselves seem anything but dark, of
course. The masonry, much of it well
preserved, is an attractive mixture of
warm pink granite, yellowish
sandstone and grey flagstone. The
roof, now open to the sky, would
have been slated.

Founded by Reginald son of
Somerled in the early 1200s, around
the same time that he established
the Abbey, the Nunnery's first
prioress was his sister Beathag. A
later prioress, Anna Maclean, died
in 1543 and from her finely carved
effigy (now in the Abbey Museum)
we catch a glimpse of how the sisters
must have looked. Over her cassock
she wore a pleated linen surplice and on
her shoulders a long robe.

Hic iacent…(Here lie…)
is all that remains of the
epitaph on this nuns'
graveslab from the late
15th century. The detail
shows two sisters in their
habits; above (not shown)
are two female figures in
lay dress, a reminder
perhaps of their
aristocratic birth.

We know virtually nothing of the young women
from the West Highland nobility who lived out their lives
here, but you can follow something of their daily round
through the buildings they left behind. Sit on the stone
benches of the chapter-house, where a chapter of the
Rule was read out each day, and walk around the cloister
garth where medicinal herbs were cultivated. To the
south is the shell of the refectory where the nuns ate and
to the west, where a road now runs, was their dormitory.
At regular intervals, day and night, they repaired to the
little church on the north side to sing psalms and pray.

From the early 1920s the Nunnery came alive again
with colour and scent when a new flower garden was laid
out and carefully tended. This was thanks to the
generosity of the Spencer family who set up a fund for
that purpose. The grounds are now looked after by a work
squad employed by the Iona Cathedral Trust.

Just before the north gate out of the Nunnery area
stands a rectangular building. This is **Teampull Rònain**, a
medieval church dedicated to St Ronan. Its existence is

West face of the 15th-century Maclean's Cross, showing a crucifix in the cross-head.

clear evidence that, alongside the religious community, there was also a local population with its own parish priest from at least the late twelfth century.

Only recently, however, have we learned that this site is very much older. Excavations in 1992 brought to light the lines of an earlier foundation, which possibly dates back to the seventh century; both below and above this were traces of dug graves. The later of these contained female and infant bones, confirming a well-documented tradition that as late as the mid-eighteenth century the island's women were buried around the Nunnery.

Before later walls enclosed it, the little white-washed structure of stone and clay would have been clearly visible from the sea. Was it where visitors or the lay folk first worshipped? Or was it a chapel for early Christian monks, a quiet retreat outside their monastic enclosure? We cannot be certain but the layers of activity over centuries imply that this was, for some reason, a special place.

Dr Johnson lamented that Iona, '…once the metropolis of learning and piety has now no school for education nor temple for worship'. In 1774, a year after his visit, this gap was partly filled when a charitable body then very active in the Highlands, the Scottish Society for the Propagation of Christian Knowledge, allocated £10 to Iona for a schoolmaster's salary. By the end of his first session he had 40 pupils on the roll, whom he taught in his own house. A school has been sited where the present one stands, directly west of the Nunnery, since about 1840 when it became a Parochial School under the control of the Church of Scotland. Since the Education Act of 1872 the school has been the responsibility of the local government council.

The scratch of pencil on slate has long given way to the hum and click of computers and the two bright, modern classrooms still provide primary education for the island's children. The pupils continue their schooling on the mainland, usually at Oban High School, returning home at weekends.

The raucous call of rooks may well accompany you up the gravel path beside the school, where tall sycamores, planted in the mid-nineteenth century, afford a rare nesting place in an island now virtually treeless.

The two buildings set back from the road here were built in 1828 as the **Parish Church** and **Manse**. Designed by Thomas Telford, they formed part of a government scheme to raise new churches in scattered, but then very populous, parishes of the Highlands and Islands. To have their own place of worship again, and their own resident minister, must have been a great event for the local congregation. For more than 200 years they had been served only intermittently by a minister based in Mull.

Rich, interleaved patterns on the east side of Maclean's Cross recall the skill of Iona's medieval craftsmen.

The site chosen bore the name of **Cill Chainnich**. Bishop William Reeves, whose edition of Adomnán is a rich source of lore, recorded that here was said to have stood a small chapel dedicated to St Kenneth, a contemporary of St Columba. Only a few tombstones of this chapel remained by the time of his visit in 1857.

From the hill behind the Parish Church, looking east to the Ross of Mull across a calm blue Sound.

The interior of the Telford church was refurbished and rearranged in 1939. It is a B-listed building and further work, particularly on the mullioned windows and the belfry, was carried out in the early 1990s. Church of Scotland services, to which visitors are welcome, are held here at 12 noon on Sundays.

Since 1985, following the linking of neighbouring parishes, the minister's main dwelling house has been at Bunessan on Mull. Vigorous fund-raising efforts by local people led to the setting up of the Iona Heritage Trust which now leases the Manse from its owners, the Church of Scotland. The upstairs floor has been adapted to provide a small flat, for the parish minister in winter and visiting ministers in summer. The downstairs area opened in 1990 as the **Iona Heritage Centre**. During the tourist season, visitors can browse through displays about island life past and present, delve into local and family history folders, study the variety of rock samples or let their offspring draw in the children's corner.

Leaving the Parish Church by the north gate and turning back down the main road you pass the tall and slender **Maclean's Cross**. Its intricate foliated designs are a fine example of the Iona carving school of the fifteenth century. In medieval times, this was a central junction where three roads met. One led from the Monastery precincts to St Ronan's Church and ran straight past the west side of the cross. Another curved round behind the Nunnery and through the present school playground to meet the first at the cross; this is assumed to be **Sraid nam Marbh** (the street of the dead) which began at Port nam Mairtear. A third short path branched off through the huddle of cottages to the landing-place at Port Rònain.

There is a narrow right-of-way through the present-day village, reached by the stile or gate just south of Maclean's Cross. It marks the boundary between the East and West Ends of the island, a division dating from the agricultural reorganisation around 1800.

The square of land between the road and the path is known as the **Gàradh Marsaili** (Marjory's enclosure), although who Marjory was has now vanished beyond recall. At one time the villagers had a right to graze a cow in the patch of ground behind their house; it was common too for a number to keep a pig and most will have planted a few potatoes. For a period, four houses – Oran Cottage, Ballymore, Shuna and Mo Dhachaidh – were each given a share of the Gàradh Marsaili when their own gardens were shortened, for reasons long since forgotten.

By the gate into the Gàradh Marsaili is a modern cairn commissioned by the National Trust for Scotland to honour the late Lord Fraser of Allander, in whose memory Sir Hugh Fraser made the purchase of

Rookery beside the Manse. In 1876, visitor C. F. G. Cumming noted that the islanders held 'devious superstitions' about the rooks, which then nested in the abbey ruins, and would not allow the birds to be molested.

Brooch design by island silversmith Alexander Ritchie (1865-1941).

the island for the nation in 1979. The walled grassy oblong just to the south was formerly the school garden, where pupils were taught the basics of horticulture.

The **village street** was where most of the crafts- and tradespeople lived last century. The 1841 census lists seven hand-loom weavers, two tailors, one shoemaker, two boat-builders, one wood-turner, one carpenter and one merchant. The last was Hugh Maclean. Two or three general stores were to operate on the island, sometimes concurrently, in the years ahead but the Macleans, in one of the row of houses at the head of the jetty, hold the record for continuity. Hugh's granddaughter, Mary Ann, ran the shop until about 1960 by which time she was well into her seventies.

The family associated most closely with weaving were the MacDonalds, one branch of whom also ran the Post Office for a while. Willie MacDonald (1902-1993) was at least the fourth generation to make Iona tweed. The old wooden loom his father, Coll, used was so big that it could not negotiate the narrow doorway of **Taigh nam Beairt** (the loom house), and had to be brought in through the window. Later Willie made a trip to Harris for training on the smaller Hattersley loom.

A relative from an earlier generation, Alexander MacDonald (1819-1887), was nicknamed 'The Mathematical Weaver'. A self-taught scholar, he often amazed visitors by jumping up from his loom to scratch out on a slate some algebraic or trigonometric problem, solving it by his own unique method.

The last on Iona to make tailoring his profession was Neil MacKay (1831-95), who had come to the island from Campbeltown as a young man and married a local girl. He took a keen interest in all aspects of island life, was an active member of the Iona Debating Society and

43

for many years acted as local correspondent for a mainland newspaper. **Taigh an Tàilleir** (the tailor's house), now called **Highland Cottage**, was long remembered as a lively ceilidh house, where MacKay's renowned grasp of news near and far, along with his celebrated wit, provided entertainment to all who dropped by.

Next door there now stands **Shuna Cottage**, presently owned by the Iona Community. It was built by Alexander and Euphemia Ritchie soon after they married in 1898. Here the Ritchies developed their Celtic Art of Iona business, designing a huge range of jewellery and other items, particularly in silver but also in brass, wood, leather and cloth. These finely crafted goods were sold from a hut just inside the south gate of the Nunnery grounds. Alex was also remembered with great affection by generations of visitors as the informed and engaging official guide to the island's sites. He and his wife both died in 1941.

The village street, bathed in warm morning light, before awakening to the bustle of the day. The Carraig Fhada (long rock), once a simple jetty, lies exposed at Port Rònain.

Am Baile Mòr, the main settlement area for many centuries, tucks neatly between the shelter of Cnoc Mòr (big hill) and the coastal fringe of vivid blue-green water.

Johnson and Boswell slept the night in a barn but clean sheets and blankets from the villagers, on top of the straw, made a 'tolerably comfortable' bed. Visitors in those days had to make do with what rough and ready accommodation the locals could provide, unless they braved their own 'tent' of oars and sail, as Thomas Pennant did. In 1798 Thomas Garnett, a professor of natural philosophy and chemistry, shared the muddy floor and leaking roof of 'a wretched hut' with various chickens, pigs and cats and was awoken by the flapping wings of a young cockerel. Luckily, his sense of humour had not deserted him; he just laughed and got up.

Sarah Murray, who explored the island in 1802, mentioned an inn where the landlady gave her a meal of fine fish and potatoes. This was probably **Iona Cottage**, which faces directly towards the landing-place. It was certainly later the home of Donald MacPhail who, when his first daughter was baptised in 1831, was entered in the register as 'innkeeper'. MacPhail was praised warmly by an American clergyman in 1849 for the simple, neat guest-room, the good peat fire and a supper of eggs, milk and freshly made oatcakes. 'How it would have spoiled the whole', he mused, 'to have come to a modern hotel with a sleek, well-fed, demure and white-aproned waiter! May the Duke of Argyll never build an Icolmkill Hotel!'

Summer tours were booming, however, and in 1867 the Duke did give permission to John MacCormick, a merchant, to raise his cottage in the centre of the village street to two storeys and open the Argyll Hotel. Luckily, a grandiose mock-Tudor design drawn up a few years earlier by London architects had been abandoned. The St Columba Hotel just north of the village and built first as a Free Church Manse, was not long behind, opening its doors to guests from 1868.

A stroll along the street on a summer's day is a pleasant diversion. Most of the houses are built of dressed granite blocks from the Ross of Mull and the rose-pink stone makes an attractive contrast with the blue-grey slate of the roofs. Thatch had largely been replaced by the middle of this century. Luxuriant pink fuschia hedges blaze from the gardens sloping to the shore. Boats bob in and out of Port Rònain. And stately white seagulls, a beady eye open for household scraps or an unguarded picnic sandwich, garrison the rocks.

Just beyond the north end of the village stands a low, granite building facing directly out to sea. Set into a niche on its seaward wall is the island's only statue of St Columba. In 1893 Alexander Chinnery-Haldane, Bishop of Argyll and the Isles, was granted a feu on which to erect a House of Prayer and Eucharist. Such was his close and enthusiastic relationship with the project that, before long, it

Statue of St Columba, looking east from the wall of the Bishop's House.

was simply being called **'The Bishop's House'**.

The plan was regarded with suspicion at the time, the local minister mounting a short-lived but spirited attack on what he regarded as an intrusion by the Episcopalians. Reputedly weary of such inter-denominational strife, the Duke of Argyll refused to withdraw permission.

The building was designed by eminent architect Alexander Ross of Inverness, who was among its first visitors in the summer of 1894. From 1896 until 1909 the House was occupied by a few members of the Society of St John the Evangelist. Known for short as the Cowley Fathers, they led simple, contemplative lives, grew vegetables and occasionally invited the locals in for tea. The House remains the property of the Episcopal Church in Scotland, operating as a retreat and guest-house for much of the year. Services are held in the small St Columba's chapel.

Iona Parish Church, erected in 1828 to the design of Thomas Telford.

The Abbey Precincts – An Eaglais Mhòr

During her Hebridean tour of 1802 Sarah Murray rode across Mull and halted 'dumb with amazement' at the Sound of Iona. From that wild shore, strewn with red granite, she could see across the water 'ruins of grandeur, that made the mind revert to ages past'. Awestruck impressions recur frequently in the accounts of early travellers and antiquarians who were rediscovering the island's sites. For the local people, too, who lived and worked alongside the ruined abbey it was *an eaglais mhòr*, 'the great church'. Great indeed it must have seemed, compared to their own small parish kirk. In English the building has always been called 'the cathedral', a status it held briefly at the end of the fifteenth century.

Had you been a pilgrim more than a thousand years before Mrs. Murray, the prospect, as you shouted across the Sound for the monks to send a coracle, would have been much more modest: a cluster of low, thatched, wooden huts above the shoreline. You approached them through an opening in the **vallum**, the raised earth boundary that surrounded the complex on three sides; on its fourth side lay the sea. A typical feature of early Irish monasteries, the vallum was not designed as a defence: it marked out the area legally occupied by the monks and symbolised their separation from the secular world.

Excavations have indicated the lines of more than one boundary on the south side, perhaps from different periods, but nothing is now visible above ground. The

Iona Abbey from the west, shortly after completion of the new pitched roof, or cap house, in November 1996, which provides improved drainage for the tower. In his gift of the historic site, it was the express wish of the 8th Duke of Argyll that this original feature of the Benedictine building be included in the renovation work.

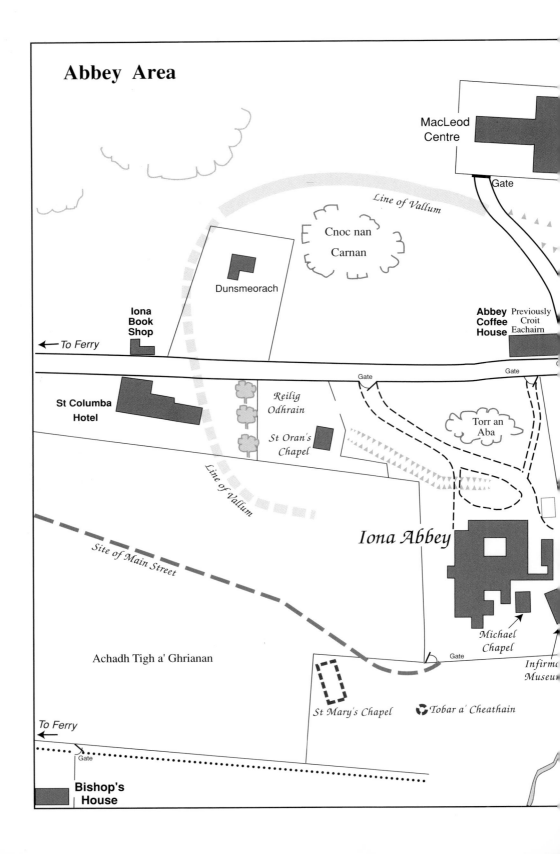

Abbey Area

MacLeod Centre

Gate

Line of Vallum

Cnoc nan Carnan

Dunsmeorach

Iona Book Shop

Abbey Coffee House — Previously Croit Eachairn

← To Ferry

Gate

Gate

St Columba Hotel

Reilig Odhrain

Torr an Aba

St Oran's Chapel

Iona Abbey

Line of Vallum

Site of Main Street

Michael Chapel

Infirmary Museum

Achadh Tigh a' Ghrianan

Gate

St Mary's Chapel

Tobar a' Cheathain

To Ferry ←

Gate

Bishop's House

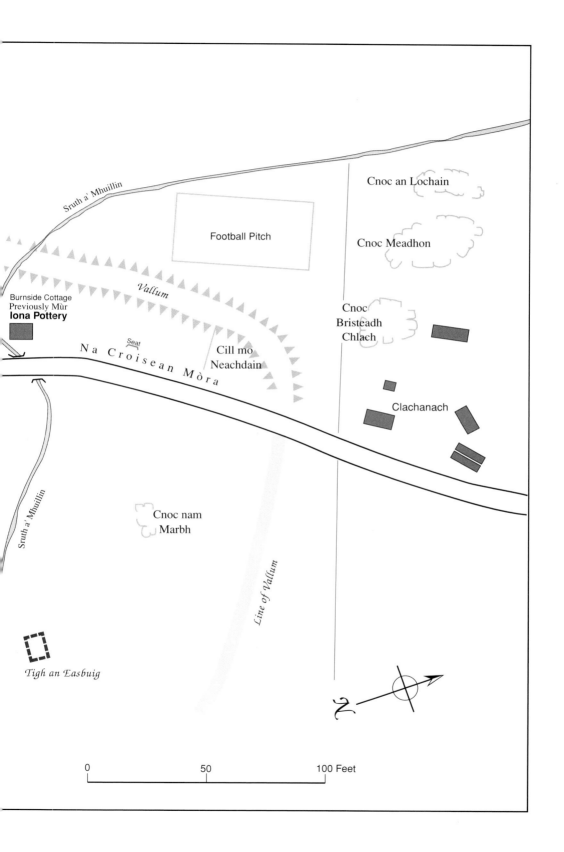

Cnoc an Lochain

Cnoc Meadhon

Sruth a' Mhuillin

Football Pitch

Vallum

Burnside Cottage
Previously Mùr
Iona Pottery

Cnoc
Bristeadh
Chlach

Seat

N a C r o i s e a n M ò r a

Cill mo
Neachdain

Clachanach

Sruth a' Mhuillin

Cnoc nam
Marbh

Line of Vallum

Tigh an Easbuig

| 0 | 50 | 100 Feet |

vallum remains much clearer to the west where it forms a broad ridge parallel to the modern road. From up here the low bump that was once the northern limit is just discernible, curving across the opposite field.

The life of the monastic community was not of course restricted to this enclosure. All over the island are places associated with the monks and their daily work and the view from the vallum, just beside the stone cottage that is now the Iona Pottery, provides one such reminder. To the west stretches **Iomair Tochair** (ridge of the causeway), a straight embankment bounding to its north a boggy area that was formerly a small loch. At 10 metres (c. 33 ft) wide, nearly 1.5 metres (c. 5 ft) high in places and solidly built of earth and boulders, this structure represents serious labour by someone. But by whom and why?

One theory links it with Cilléne Droichtech, an eighth century abbot whose name means 'bridge-builder' and who was an anchorite or recluse. Did he make the causeway for easier access to the seclusion of the hills? Others prefer to speculate that it was a water-meadow dam, flooding and draining the area for winter pasture, or simply a mill-dam.

For, beside the Pottery, runs **Sruth a' Mhuillin** (the mill burn) by whose banks there must have been regular activity to dry and grind corn for the Monastery's daily bread. Traces of what may have been a timber-built mill undercroft have been found by the burn, very close to where it cuts through the vallum, and eighteenth-century travellers reported the remains of a mill and a kiln in this vicinity. In earlier centuries, stone-built horizontal mills may have been more likely and Adomnán also refers to the use of hand querns.

The Early Christian Monastery's prime tasks, however, were carried out in the settlement at the heart of the vallum. In their cells monks copied and illuminated the psalms until the clang of a hand bell called them to worship in their simple church. Nothing can be seen today of these buildings, so impermanent was their construction. Moreover, the later medieval Monastery took over part or all of the same site.

Stained glass window of St Columba, placed in the north transept of the Abbey church in 1965. Designed by William Wilson, it was dedicated to the Revd Kenneth Macleod (1873-1955) who had life-long links with the Hebrides, particularly with the islands of Eigg, where he grew up, and Gigha, which was his last charge. He often visited Iona.

COLUM CILLE

Remember in the LORD
the Rev Kenneth MacLeod
D.D. Pastor and Bard

So long as the songs
of the Gael are sung
this name will
endure 1873-1955

W. Wilson 1965.

N

| 0 | 10 | 20 | 30 | 40 | 50 | 60 | feet |
| 0 | | 10 | | 20 | | 30 | 40 metres |

ABBEY PLAN KEY

1	West Door	12	Sculpture by Jacques Lipchitz
2	Watch-Tower	13	Chapter-House (Library and
3	St Columba's Shrine		Dormitory above)
4	Nave	14	Iona Community Shop (Refectory
5	Crossing		above)
6	North Transept	15	West Range
7	South Transept	16	Iona Community Office
8	Choir	17	Abbot's House
9	South Choir Aisle	18	Reredorter
10	Sacristy	19	The Michael Chapel
11	Cloisters	20	Museum, formerly the Infirmary

One spot alone may allow us to stand briefly in the shoes of Columba himself. The rocky hillock of **Tòrr an Aba** (the abbot's knoll) meets Adomnán's description of the saint's wooden writing hut as being in an elevated position. Later stone foundations have now been exposed on the top of the knoll and signs of a medieval cross-base show that it was considered a special place. Here then, perhaps, was where a clumsy visitor tipped over the little ink-horn as Adomnán relates; traces of holly, from whose leaves ink was made, were identified during excavation of a ditch nearby. And here Columba was working on the thirty-fourth psalm on 9 June 597, the night he died.

Events of considerable importance unfolded within sight of Tòrr an Aba during the decades before and after Columba's death. Somewhere below here, in 574, he consecrated Aedán son of Gabrán as king of Dál Riata, one of the earliest such ceremonies in Europe. For a period after about 616 Oswald, a prince of Northumbria, lived in exile among the monks of Iona. After regaining his throne he sent for one of them, also Aedán, to be ordained bishop of a new monastery on Lindisfarne. In 664, however, the delegation which returned from the Synod of Whitby brought dispiriting news to the huts within the vallum. The expanding Northumbrian community had elected to conform with aspects of Roman liturgical practice, thus signalling an end to political and spiritual control from Iona.

As generation succeeded generation on the island itself, the brothers were probably buried close to their church according to the custom of the times. The first recorded burial within the community was that of an unnamed Briton, a pilgrim from the part of the south-west mainland then known as Strathclyde. Adomnán describes the vision Columba had of this man's soul ascending to heaven.

Nowhere in Adomnán, however, is the legend of Oran. This elusive figure is said to have been buried alive in order to consecrate the first monastery's ground and his name lives on in the island's main graveyard, the **Reilig Odhráin**. But who was he? A list of those who came with

Columba from Ireland is attached to one of the Adomnán manuscripts; no 'Oran' is among them. Adomnán does refer to a contemporary of his own, one Máel Odrain (devotee of Odran or Oran), thus implying that a saint of that name existed at some time but it is not clear when.

The linking of human sacrifice with the Columban story is quite late, dating only from the twelfth century. By the seventeenth, oral tradition had apparently added a twist: the grave was re-opened and Oran gave a lively account of the other world. Shocked by such sacrilege, so the tale goes, Columba ordered that earth be heaped onto the offending mouth to silence it forever. Burial alive is a not uncommon theme in pagan legend yet somehow it became attached to this spot close to a wellspring of the Christian faith.

The graveyard has a quiet and dignified atmosphere, a place to be respected above all as one where the local community still buries its dead. The area may have been set aside initially as a burial-ground for lay folk but, as Iona's prestige grew, the island's very soil came to be regarded as sacred. Among these stones, therefore, local and national history are irrevocably intertwined. Here are remembered generations of islanders, along with rulers of the early kingdom of the Scots and, later, chiefs from powerful West Highland families. The names of some are known, while many more have long lain in anonymity. A slab of red granite, incised with a single cross, has been traditionally associated with a French king or nobleman but who he was we cannot tell. The oldest decipherable local inscription is for a John MacKay, simply 'Tenant of Icolmkill'. He and his wife Margaret Bell were both born in 1730.

In 1882 the US Consul, Bret Harte, was astonished to hear the local guide point out the graves of 15 American sailors, drowned in a shipwreck less than 20 years before. (The story is told in chapter 9.) He arranged for an obelisk to be erected near the east wall, to honour their memory and that of the islanders who tried to save them. Also claimed by the sea, but unnamed, are several sailors from two world wars, washed up on the island's shore.

From Torr an Aba, perhaps the site of Columba's cell. Low sunlight and shadow streak the seaward side of Reilig Odhráin, Iona's historic burial-ground. The triangular area to the left is a modern extension, created less than 20 years ago.

The people of South Uist thought so highly of their young doctor, Donald Black, that when he died in 1885 they raised money for a tombstone in his native Iona. The wider Scottish public funded a stone designed by artist John Duncan to the memory of *Marsaili nan Oran* (Marjory of the Songs). Collector and performer of Hebridean melodies, Marjory Kennedy Fraser was a regular visitor to the island and her ashes were brought here by a large crowd of her admirers in 1932.

Local minister Donald McVean defected to the new Free Church in 1843 and was forced to preach from a kind of wooden sentry-box in the very grounds of the **Reilig Odhráin**, before he got permission to build a church. Now his family grave lies snug against the south wall of the chapel.

Had you stepped off a boat early last century, you would have been led around these graves by a small, spry, voluble man, one of the island's great characters. For over 50 years Alan Maclean was the schoolmaster and guide or, as a visitor in 1832 quaintly put it, 'the village pedagogue, mystagogue and antiquary' from whom 'legendary tales' might be had for sixpence! He died in 1853 aged 92 and some years later a relative from Tobermory raised an obelisk in his memory near to the centre of the graveyard.

The appearance of the Reilig Odhráin has changed much over the centuries. In the large socket-stone to the south of the chapel a free-standing carved cross may, perhaps, have marked an entrance through the vallum. There is no way of knowing how the tombstones, great or humble, were first arranged. Over centuries they were re-used for later burials, dug up or damaged by curious scholars until, in 1858, the finest of them were gathered into two rows and railed off.

The two railed enclosures, known as the Ridge of the Kings and the Ridge of the Chiefs, were popular with visitors and featured in many postcards and press photographs. The names were a little misleading, however. It has certainly been possible to identify some of the chiefs' stones from their inscriptions: Angus, son of Lord MacDonald of Islay, for example; Colum, son of Ruairi MacLeod; Gilbride MacKinnon; John MacIan of Ardnamurchan. In contrast, no stones can be assigned to particular kings. Up until the late eighteenth century observant visitors could still spy, through the undergrowth by then rampant, the remains of three cell-like shrines which were believed to shelter the tombs of Scots, Irish and Norse royalty respectively. Yet neither names nor numbers can be quoted with confidence as the main sources – lists of early Pictish and Scottish kings – are notoriously unreliable, being riven with error and contradiction.

None of this, however, undermines

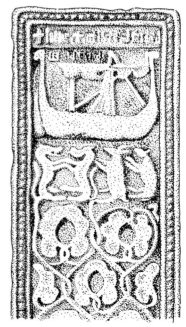

'Here lies Colum, son of Ruari MacLeod' is inscribed on this fine, early 16th-century, carved slab of the Iona school. Ruari was a chief of the MacLeods of Lewis.

Doorway of St Oran's Chapel, with chevron and beak-head decoration typical of the late 12th-century Irish style.

the status Iona undoubtedly held throughout medieval Gaeldom and, earlier, during the forging of the Scottish kingdom. It was a place of significance and sanctity and to be buried there was considered a high honour.

Wary of increased risks from twentieth-century air pollution, the Iona Cathedral Trust has now brought most of the stones under cover – in St Oran's Chapel, in the Abbey church and cloisters and in the Abbey Museum.

St Oran's Chapel is the oldest of Iona's surviving ecclesiastical monuments and dates from the late twelfth century. The ornamentation on the round-arched doorway is characteristic of the Irish style of that period. Re-roofed in 1957, the interior is cool and simply furnished. The most probable origin of the building is as a mortuary chapel for the MacDonald family, founders of the Lordship of the Isles.

Graveslabs lie underfoot and on the south wall rises an elaborate tomb-recess. From among the stone foliage decorating the lower arch peeks a 'green man', a kind of grotesque human face, now much eroded. At the apex above him is the head of a bishop, complete with mitre, and at the very top is a carved crucifix. Who exactly this was for is not certain, but records do cite the chapel as the burial-place for both John and Donald MacDonald, first and second Lords of the Isles. According to clan historians, the proper ceremony due a great chief was observed for John in 1380 when the abbot and all his clergy came out to meet the funeral party and conducted services over eight days and nights.

From Martyrs' Bay coffins were borne to the Reilig Odhráin along a paved cause-way known as **Sràid nam**

Marbh (the street of the dead; see chapter 8). This street has long been destroyed or built over but a continuation of it, of similar construction, now lies exposed leading from the north wall of the graveyard towards the Abbey precincts.

The grassy area just west of the Abbey buildings holds much of interest, spanning various periods in the island's religious history. An attractive, paved seating area, planted out with flowers, has been created on the site of the medieval brewhouse and bakery. The white doves fluttering nearby are not merely a modern photogenic flourish; a dovecote was found to be incorporated in the church tower.

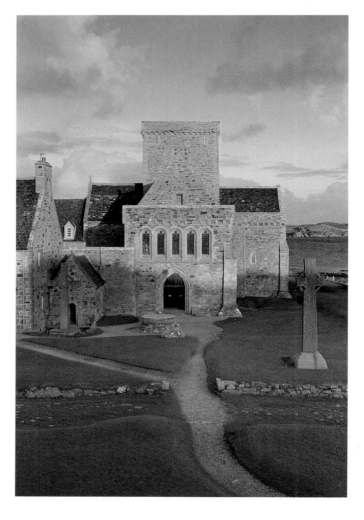

The old familiar shape of Iona Abbey, before the new roof was added to its tower in 1996. The restored church and nave have been in use since 1910 but repairs and conservation work, such as repointing of masonry, remain ongoing and vital tasks.

The tiny chapel jutting out to the north of the main entrance has come to be known as **St Columba's Shrine**, from the strong tradition that it was erected over the saint's burial place. The foundations, which were all that remained before restoration in 1962, showed that the chapel originally stood apart and its size and style place it towards the end of the Early Christian era. It was probably on this doorstep that King Magnus Barelegs of Norway, on a Hebridean expedition in 1098, was stopped in his tracks. According to the saga, reverence for whatever lay within caused him to close the door again and order that none should enter. The chapel is now a quiet place for private prayer or meditation.

The existence of this small oratory and the siting of three **high crosses** nearby strengthen the assumption that the same approximate area was used by succeeding monastic communities, from Columba's day up until the Benedictine house was established around 1200. It was customary in the early Irish church to mark the site of signficant events with a wooden cross or a plain stone on which a cross was cut. Adomnán records several such examples on Iona.

By the eighth century, when the earliest of the larger free-standing crosses were carved, their function had grown to embrace the ceremonial, as part of a processional route and as a focus for meditation. The broken shaft of **St Matthew's Cross** has been removed to the shelter of the museum. There, too, are the original fragments of **St John's Cross**, skilfully reconstructed to its impressive overall height of 5.3 metres (c. 17 ft). Since 1970 an exact concrete replica set into the base outside St Columba's Shrine has been a remarkably acceptable substitute.

Only **St Martin's Cross** stands where it was first erected. Crafted from a single block of grey epidiorite, it has weathered the storms of well over a thousand years. The east face is carved in heavy relief, the patterns of round bosses encircled by serpents and, at the top, lion-like creatures. At the centre of the west face are depicted the Virgin and Child and the figure-scenes below have been tentatively interpreted as Biblical in inspiration: Daniel and the lions, David playing his harp, Abraham and Isaac.

From surviving shaft and base fragments, and from place-name evidence, it is fair to assume that a number of other free-standing crosses once graced the landscape. One or two must have been sited at **Na Croisean Mòra** (the big crosses), an old name for the grassy bank below the vallum just north of the mill-burn, and in **Parc nan Croisean** (park of the crosses), south of the St Columba Hotel. Reports of hundreds of such crosses, cast into the sea by zealots of the Reformation, have been wildly exaggerated. They can be traced to that old culprit, a slip of the pen, when a seventeenth-century note about 300 incised crosses – very different – was wrongly interpreted.

Directly in front of the main west door to the Abbey is the round parapet of a man-made well, long known to the islanders as a reliable source of water even in the driest season. It seems to have been constructed towards the end of the occupation of the Abbey in the sixteenth century. Dr Johnson was offered a drink from 'St Columba's Well' but, if this was it, proximity to the traditional burial place of the saint is the likely reason for that description. It was not a regular name for this or any other well on Iona, which is curious, for there are many wells dedicated to Columba elsewhere in Scotland and Ireland.

Between the Abbey and the shore there is a natural spring, now covered over, called **Tobar a' Cheathain**. The name is obscure but it may mean the well dedicated to someone called 'Ceathan'. Long reputed locally to have healing powers, it was even celebrated in verse in *Lumsden & Sons Steamboat Companion*, an early guidebook: *S cha mho dh'iarr e ri ol, Ach uisge mòr a Cheathain* – 'Nor did he want to drink anything but the good water of Ceathan'.

Water was often endowed with unusual powers in traditional lore. The granite trough, incised with a cross, by the main door into the Abbey church was where pilgrims washed their feet before entering. For locals, however, it was 'the cradle of the north wind' where they could conjure up a breeze whenever it was needed.

Stones too were special. Boswell was directed to a greyish coloured slab sunk in the earth where he made a secret and solemn vow, as was the custom. Other

St John's Cross. Much of the stone was brought from the Argyll mainland and the craftsmen who laboured over the serpent-and-boss and spiral decoration seen in this detail may have been Irish or, indeed, Pictish. It is thought that the ring is a later addition, invented to strengthen the wide arms.

accounts of this so-called 'Black Stone', upon which oaths were binding, imply that a figure was carved on it. It was reputedly smashed to pieces early last century.

The shallow bowl, perhaps the fragment of a quern, which held the Clachan Bràth, or Judgement Stones, may survive. Now in the Abbey museum, it lay for many years close to St Oran's Chapel and was identified locally as such. It once held three round stones – 'noble globes of white marble' according to Dr Sacheverell in 1688 – which visitors were invited to turn sunwise. Once the basin was worn away by this action, they were also told, the Day of Judgement would be nigh. John MacCulloch, a friend of Sir Walter Scott, cannot have been the only one to wonder drily, in 1824, what was the attraction of hastening such an event.

As visitors go into the Abbey by its big west door, two things may be obvious. This is no longer a working monastery and so no brothers go about their daily round as happens in some other restored abbeys. But nor is it a quiet, deserted monument. There is often a bustle about the place, for the adjoining living quarters are leased to the Iona Community, whose staff occupy them all year round and who receive groups and conferences there for much of the year. They also run a shop, a coffee-house and the MacLeod Centre, a purpose-built facility which caters particularly for young people, families and the disabled. The Community's daily services, at 9am and

Granite footbath, also once known in local lore as the cradle of the north wind.

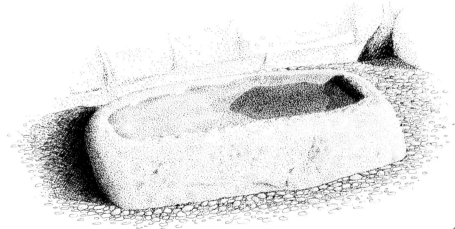

63

9pm, and Holy Communion at 10.30am on Sundays, are
ecumenical and are open to anyone staying on the island.

Over the three centuries after 1200 the Benedictine
Abbey was expanded and reconstructed several times.
Clues to some of these stages can be easily seen in the
interior: where a flat roof, rather than the modern
vaulted one, covered the choir, for example, or where the
floor level was once higher, giving way to an undercroft
below. From outside, however, the restored buildings
today look largely as they might have done at the end of
the fifteenth century.

Modern efforts to reclaim the Abbey's former glory
date back to the mid-nineteenth century when the
Society of Antiquaries brought pressure on the Duke of
Argyll to carry out some minimal repairs. In the late
1870s important renovation work was done, directed by
the architect R. Rowand Anderson, to strengthen walls
and conserve stonework.

After the setting up of the Iona Cathedral Trust, the
first phase of serious rebuilding (1902-5) saw the choir,
crossing and transepts reroofed under the guidance of
Thomas Ross and John Honeyman. In 1909-10 the walls
of the nave rose again, from ground-level for the most
part, to the design of P. MacGregor Chalmers. The
reconstruction of the cloisters, chapter-house, refectory
and other monastic buildings came under the direction of
architect Ian G. Lindsay between 1939 and 1965.

Yet in spite of the various minds and hands at work
over such a span of time, it is hard for the layperson to
spot where medieval stonework meets that of this
century. Thanks to the skill of the different teams of
masons and the consistency of the materials used, the
whole complex has a pleasing uniformity. Inside, the
pattern of pink and grey stone appears time-worn with
age, but in a sense it is quite modern. In the days when
the monks processed in for their daily offices the walls
would have been lime-washed white and, very probably,
bright with mural painting.

Everywhere within the Abbey church and its

Rounded granite cobbles pave the Street of the Dead, flanked by the doughty, thousand-year-old St Martin's Cross. The shadow of St John's Cross, behind, falls on the end of the West Range, the last part of the monastic sites to be rebuilt, in 1965, by the Iona Community.

outbuildings old and new come together. The west doorway, and the small watch-tower for a door-keeper, date from the fifteenth century, while immediately inside the entrance stands a baptismal font of Iona marble, gifted in 1913. The fabric and furnishings of the building commemorate numerous people and bodies who supported the modern restoration, including the Highlanders of Nova Scotia who funded the large south window of the nave and, notably, Helen Campbell of Blythswood. It was she who, almost single-handedly, mobilised Woman's Guilds from the Church of Scotland to raise the money to rebuild the nave in 1909-10. A much more recent dedication, made in 1991, is that for new lighting by which Ralph and Jenny Morton, early members of the Iona Community, are remembered.

Set into the floor of the nave are memorials from a far earlier time: small incised crosses mark burial sites uncovered during work on the foundations. Pebbles found in two of these – recording, perhaps, the ages or years in

holy orders of the long-forgotten brothers – were placed
in the paving slabs above.

On the left of the crossing, at the heart of the
cruciform building, is a handsome oak screen. This was
the gift of the Queen, on her visit to the island in 1956.
Behind it lies the north transept which is the oldest part
of the whole complex, surviving largely unscathed since
the first Benedictine structure of the early 1200s. From
here, later, led the night stair from the sleeping quarters.
As the monks filed silently down for the nocturnal
offices, they passed beneath a depiction of the
Temptation in the Garden of Eden, carved on a west
capital of the crossing-arch.

Opposite, below the arch between the south transept
and south aisle, Adam and Eve reappear in the Fall, their
fate sealed by the figure of a sword-bearing angel. All the
carved capitals on the south crossing-arch and along the
aisle are worthy of a look for their fine ornamentation
and lively scenes: strange beasts and birds,
intertwined with foliage; monstrous demons and
biblical figures; a warrior on horseback; three
men about to sacrifice a cow. From the west
crossing-arch high above a face looks down,
apparently frozen in an eternal grimace.

An inscription on one of these
capitals, though now partly effaced, brings
a directly personal touch: *Donaldus O
Brolchan fecit hoc opus* – 'Donald Ò
Brolchán made this work'. This
member of a family linked to the
monastery at Derry must have been
a master-mason here in the
fifteenth century. And he may
have settled on the island, for
two Ò Brolchán men are
named in a document about
Iona of 1716.

In the south transept
are effigies of the eighth

Head from the stone
effigy of Abbot John
MacKinnon (1467-c.1498).

Stone gargoyle
grimaces from the west
crossing-arch.

Duke of Argyll and his third wife, Ina McNeill of Colonsay, sculpted from white Carrara marble by Sir George Frampton. The Duchess's casket was laid to rest below her statue in 1925. The Duke had been buried in the family graveyard at Kilmun in 1900 but this memorial is a reminder of his family's long association with the historic sites of Iona. Nearby hangs a copy of the deed whereby he handed over the buildings into the care of the Iona Cathedral Trust.

The communion table at the east end of the choir was designed by P. MacGregor Chalmers and installed around 1917. Like its medieval predecessor, it is of greenish-white Iona marble. On either side two more figures lie motionless, in bold relief. That on the right is attributed to Abbot Dominic under whose administration (1421-c.1465) an earlier period of profligacy and neglect was curbed and major repairs to the Abbey undertaken. On the left is the effigy of a successor, Abbot John MacKinnon (1467-c.1498), son of Lachlan, chief of the clan. Both effigies are clothed in full Eucharistic vestments and that of Abbot MacKinnon remains in particularly fine condition.

Unseen now beneath a modern Persian carpet on the altar-step is a slab of Tournai marble that once gleamed with brass inlay in the outline of an armoured man. At nearly 1.8 metres (6 ft) in length, and in such a prominent position, this must have been an impressive memorial indeed. It is thought most likely to have been made for one of the Macleans of Duart in the late fourteenth century.

Two doors lead from the Abbey nave into the cloisters, whose grassy garth contrasts brightly with the cool grey of the surrounds. The bronze sculpture of

the Virgin was either loved or hated when it was placed in the centre of the completed square in 1959. But for its Lithuanian creator, Jacques Lipchitz, it symbolised 'The Descent of the Spirit' and the modern piece has become, for many, a familiar fixture in its much older setting. The reconstructed double columns of the arcade openings incorporate two original pairs and gradually over the years since 1959, the capitals have been delicately ornamented by stone-carver Chris Hall. They depict flowers and birds of Iona as well as plants from throughout Britain and from the Holy Land.

A rounded late medieval doorway indicates the entrance to the chapter-house and above here is a room assumed to have been the monks' library. It has been restored as such, largely due to the generosity of a local man, the Revd Robert L. Ritchie, who bequeathed his own collection of Gaelic and religious texts in 1934. His brother Alex also donated books and funds and their wish was that the library be for the benefit of islanders and

A quiet moment in the Abbey Church (right) before evening service. Candles glimmer on the crossing floor and daffodils are bright against the dark wood of the choir stalls. Meanwhile, glimpsed through the columns of the floodlit cloisters (above), the bronze Virgin supports a cross of yellow flowers, heralding the Iona Community's Easter celebration.

scholars with an interest in Highland
or church history.

Turning right out of the
main exit from the cloisters, and
continuing round the outside,
you reach two buildings of great
interest and beauty. In the
Abbey Museum, on the probable
site of the Benedictines' infirmary,
are displayed St Oran's Cross and the
original St John's Cross along with a range of
carved stones from Early Christian through to medieval
times. Further slabs are on view round the cloisters and at
the west end of the Abbey nave.

All that remains of
Tigh an Easbuig, home to
the Bishop of the Isles in
the early 16th century.

The whole Iona collection is of outstanding richness.
It has been comprehensively documented by the Royal
Commission on the Ancient and Historical Monuments
of Scotland, whose series of volumes on Argyll includes
one devoted entirely to Iona. What Iona craftsmen of the
past have left behind is a tangible reminder of the island's
long-held cultural and spiritual importance.

The little chapel to the south, of typical West
Highland style, was named the **Michael Chapel** upon its
restoration in 1959. There had been a building dedicated
to St Michael – Bishop John Campbell had it re-roofed in
the 1580s in preparation for his own burial place – and
Walker, in 1764, referred to 'the Chapells of several
different saints' on the island. It has been simply and
attractively refurbished.

Visible from the east end of the Abbey complex are
the ruined fragments of another early sanctuary, **St Mary's
Chapel**. This one was probably erected during the
thirteenth century and its function may have been
primarily to receive pilgrims on their way from the
landing place to the Abbey.

In the field just north of the mill-burn can be seen a
single arch, also built predominantly of rose-pink granite
boulders held by lime-mortar. This is the surviving
middle wall of **Tigh an Easbuig** (the Bishop's House),

which must date from some time after a papal decree of 1499 brought together the abbacy of Iona and the bishopric of the Isles. Two-storeyed, with a hall nearly 8 metres (26 ft) long and a chimney in the west gable, it will have been an impressive building compared to the low dwellings of most of the population of the time. Bishops of the Isles will have used the house in turn, some of them as a residence and others to receive visitors or discuss ecclesiastical business.

It is not impossible that here was the court set up by Andrew Knox, Bishop of the Isles, in 1609, at which nine Gaelic chiefs assented to the Statutes of Iona. This set of conditions, drawn up by James VI, covered, among other things, a limit on the bearing of firearms and the size of the chiefs' households, a curb on liquor importation and on the free movement of bards and vagabonds, and a requirement to educate children in English. They were a key part of prolonged efforts by the monarchy to subdue what were seen as the lawless regions of the realm and gradually draw their leaders into lowland society.

That the king summonsed the chiefs to Iona is a reminder of the island's enduring sanctity. Any oath sworn there was considered binding. But the Statutes were to have profound repercussions on the fate of Gaeldom and its culture. It is ironic that they were enacted within sight of the very spot where Gaelic language and learning had put down such strong early roots.

Ruins of the 13th-century St Mary's Chapel, with the restored abbey beyond.

The East End

At the making of the crofts around 1802, the fifth Duke of Argyll divided the tenantry into two townships: the East End and the West End. At first sight this may appear a little odd, as the island lies on a north-east/south-west axis, but the designation stuck. The East End has remained the common local description for all the land north-east of the Abbey grounds.

As you cross the burn going north, a broad field on the right stretches towards the sea. This now forms part of the St Columba farm but, until the mid nineteenth century, it was the arable land allocated to two crofting families. Before the days of fencing, keeping cattle off the growing crops or herding them into enclosures near the houses at night were time-consuming occupations. These tasks frequently fell to children, of course, but one particular family also acted as township herds. The last of these in the East End, before they emigrated to Canada, were MacEacherns and a patch of ground south of the burn – where the Abbey Coffee House now stands – is remembered as **Croit Eachairn** (MacEachern's croft).

On the left of the road, just by the curve of the vallum's northern limit, the outline of a house and outbuildings can be traced in the grass. The stone oblong is not large, about 5.5 metres by 1.8 metres (18 ft by 6 ft); but it will have been typical of the people's dark, smoky, cramped dwellings, often shared with hens and a beast or two, before improvements such as gable chimneys and glazed windows came in towards the end of the nineteenth century. A family of Camerons lived here but, one day in the 1830s, they left for Australia. This was a decade before the big waves of emigration, and before official records were kept, but their neighbours over the wall remembered their going and passed down their name.

The view due east from Dun I, towards the pink granite of Kentra point on the Ross of Mull and the dark crags of Burg behind. The fields at the foot of the hill had to support four families in the middle of the nineteenth century. The broad emerald furrows they once tilled are now grazed by ewes and lambs.

Also nearby, on the corner of the vallum itself, a triangular patch of grass conceals some even more poignant story. Its name, **Cill mo Neachdain**, is obscure but local belief is that it was a small graveyard. Whether this was the empty ground for the burial of murderers and unbaptised children, described rather vaguely by Martin Martin in 1695 as 'between the Church and the gardens', cannot be certain. But a saying in circulation into this century does conjure up the tragedy of violence or infant mortality: *'Thiodhlaic mi mo naoi nighnean mar sheachdnar an Cill mo Neachdain ann an I'* – 'I buried my nine

Incised stone found at Cladh an Diseirt and now labelled 'St Columba's Pillow'.

daughters as seven here', the voice tells us, meaning presumably that two or even three of the sisters died, and were laid to rest, together.

Beside the road stands **The Duchess's Cross,** erected in 1878 to the memory of Elizabeth, first wife of the eighth Duke of Argyll. The granite was supplied by William Vass from his small quarry at Deargphort, almost opposite on the Ross of Mull.

The seat here offers a good vantage point across the green eastern slopes of the island. Near the foot of the field below the cross lies **Cladh an Diseirt**, meaning the burial place of the hermitage, although it has an alternative name, **Cladh Iain**, burial place of, or dedicated to, John. Never fully excavated, its origins are not certain but it does contain a rectangular foundation of the dimensions of a small medieval chapel. The site is a Scheduled Ancient Monument.

Speculation was rife in the 1870s that this might in turn hide a much older, even a Columban, site when a stone with an incised cross was found there. Chance alone brought this to light after crofter Dugald MacArthur felt something bump his wheel each time he carted seaweed up from the shore for his crops. Finally, he dug the offending article up. Antiquarians of the period were excited. Could this be the pillow-stone which Adomnán said was a marker at the saint's grave? No-one can be sure but, ever since, the oval stone now in the Abbey Museum has been labelled 'St Columba's Pillow'.

Following up this line of thought, and without the benefit of later archaeological surveys, one or two enthusiasts of the late nineteenth century proposed that the Columban monastery was located near to Cladh an

Diseirt. There was a romantic notion too that a flat-topped granite boulder nearby was 'Columba's Table', where the monks ate. They would have had to be very tall for, towering 1.8 metres (6 ft) above the ground, it is not called the Clach Mhòr (big stone) for nothing!

The road either side of the Duchess's Cross runs along the top of the raised beach, formed in post-glacial times, and is called **Iomair na h-Achd** (Ridge of the Act). According to an account written by a local man in 1848, this was where 'a great assembly of all the chiefs in the isles...fixed their tents upon a ridge of gravily land...the statute ridge'. This was the camp, in other words, for followers of the nine island chiefs who had come to sign the Statutes of Iona (described in the previous chapter). This local tradition might merely be an imaginative interpretation, 200 years on, of a place-name whose origins had been lost. But those few days in August 1609 may well have been a boisterous and colourful event, talked about for years afterwards. It is an

Highland calf contentedly at home on the flower-rich turf above Traigh Bàn nam Manach at the north end of the island.

Telephone lines follow the curve of the road, heading north just past Cnoc Cùil Phàil croft house.

intriguing, and by no means impossible, notion.

Dun I (pronounced 'dun-ee' and not 'dun-one'!) at 101 m (332 ft) is the island's highest hill. It provides grazing ground for Achabhaich croft and a rough path leads part of the way up from the field behind the house. The summit offers a superb panorama on a clear day. Out beyond the low lines of Tiree and Coll you might see the hills of Barra and South Uist. To the north, behind the line of black geometrical shapes that mark the Treshnish Isles and Staffa, rise the peaks of Rum and Eigg and, between them, if you are lucky, the Cuillins of Skye. From the north-east the vista swings across the blue stepped ridges of Ulva and the Burg headland of Mull with, perhaps, the smooth summit of Ben More above, and round to the red granite archipelago of the Ross. To the south-east lie Colonsay and Oronsay, with the Paps of Jura beyond and the grey-green Rhinns of Islay to the right.

Two lighthouses wink on the horizon: Skerryvore on the reef south-west of Tiree and Dubh Artach, guarding

the treacherous Torran Rocks off the Ross of Mull.
Completed in 1844 and 1872 respectively, their beacons
did much to reduce the high toll of shipwrecks in these
waters.

The remains of a
circular grain kiln, just
north of Achabhaich
croft boundary.

Several times Adomnán depicts Columba as
retreating for contemplation to various quiet places, one
of them the *munitio magna* (great fort or hill). From there,
once, the saint saw a great storm-cloud in the north
heralding a terrible plague. As the most prominent point
on Iona, this spot is very likely to have been Dun I.

The cairn on the summit has been much depleted in
recent years. It was built, to a height of over 1.8 metres
(6 ft), to commemorate Queen Victoria's Diamond
Jubilee in 1897. On that occasion, and on other notable
anniversaries or celebrations, a bonfire was held on Dun
I. It was customary for the oldest islander present to light
the first spark. Just east of the cairn is an Ordnance
Survey trig point.

About 55 metres (180 ft) from the cairn, due north,
is a rock pool called **Tobar na h-Aois** (Well of Age).
Bathe your face three times here at sunrise, runs an old
belief, and youth will be magically restored.

Continuing north on the road, a circular heap of

stones is clearly visible in the first field on the left. This once functioned as an *àtha* or kiln, essential in the damp Hebridean climate for drying corn before it was ground. There must have been others on the island but this is the only spot where both the name, and a few traces overground, have survived.

Iona's location, partly encircled as it is by a patchwork of other islands, is a major contributory factor to one of its best known scenes. As you approach the dazzling white sands at the north-east corner, the appeal to artists over the years is obvious: varied shapes and colours in the middle and far landscape; a mixture of turf, rock and shore at your feet; and, under the ever-changing Hebridean sky, the peacock blues and greens of the shallow waters between. **Traigh Bàn nam Manach** (white strand of the monks) has long been a favoured spot to set up an easel. Many of the painters who came regularly to the island in the early decades of the twentieth century would gravitate to the north end, with its splendid views across to Mull. For a time one particular rock used to be daubed with colour every summer from the daily cleaning of their brushes. Two of the best known members of the group known as the Scottish Colourists became closely associated with Iona, Francis C B Cadell first visiting in 1912 and Samuel J Peploe in 1920.

About the middle of the grassland above Traigh Bàn is a fresh-water spring called **Tobar Magh Luinge** (St Moluag's Well). This dedication speeds us right back to the sixth century when Moluag from Bangor established his monastery on Lismore in the Firth of Lorn. There was said to be a friendly rivalry between him and St Columba.

The north coast of Iona saw traffic of various sorts to and from the seas. The strand's name recalls the troubled years of the early ninth century when the

Skylark. A divinity student on retreat in 1926 wrote of Iona: '...the most wonderful thing about it is the song of the skylark, I think there must be hundreds of them...'.

79

Norse harried and plundered the west coast. The brothers, setting out to receive the high-prowed boats spied surging from the north, would have been defenceless. Tradition claims that, in one of these encounters, the monks were slain where they stood on this pure white beach.

Calm and contemplation now prevail near this once unquiet spot. By the shore is a small retreat-house owned by the Findhorn Foundation, some of whose members also live on the nearby island of Erraid off the tip of the Ross of Mull.

If you wander back south along the sands, you come to **Port na Fraing** (bay of the Frenchman). Whether the name originated with a shipwrecked mariner from the continent or if it has something to do with the mysterious French nobleman buried in the Reilig Odhráin, no-one knows. It is a narrow, relatively sheltered creek and was much used by locals and by the Fionnphort ferryman in the days of sail, if he had to tack north under a stiff

A still, silvery sea reaches from the white sands at the north-east tip of Iona (above), across to the mouth of Loch Scridain in Mull, where clouds mask the higher hills. From the summit of Dun I (right), north Mull and Ulva merge into a hazy blue background while at Lagandorain, below, a ploughed field waits for the new season's crop.

breeze. There are a couple of boat noosts, hollows cut into the bank where boats could be drawn up in safety.

A huge granite erratic appears to balance near the water's edge and, a few steps to the north, is a smaller, greyish rock slightly concave on its landward side. This is a ringing rock, producing several different notes when struck sharply with a stone. It was usual to leave a pebble for that purpose in the hollow – which may or may not be a man-made cup-mark – near the top.

From Traigh Bàn nam Manach there is a good walk, on short-cropped sandy turf, across the north end of the island. The sands here, **Traigh an t-Suidhe** (beach of the seat) and **Traigh na Crìche** (beach of the boundary) are also magnificent. They are very exposed and marram grass has been planted in the dunes at various stages, in an effort to stem erosion. The 'boundary' in one of the names may refer to the area known as **Calva** which takes its name from the nearby Eilean Chalbha (Calf island).

Here were allocated the furthest two crofts in the East End. Broad rigs undulate underfoot but, apart from a portion brought back under the plough during both the First and Second World Wars, the ground here has not been cultivated since the last family, MacDonalds, emigrated to Canada in 1888.

Here on the edge of the ocean they had worked 13 acres of arable land. An *Oban Times* report from 1912 tells us that in Manitoba one generation later, on the holding they named Iona Farm, the same family had 500 acres under crop and raised 26,000 bushels of wheat. It was indeed the New World. Today the footings of their two houses, and the adjoining yards for stock and fodder, have shrunk into the grass above the beach. Behind a

Otters can sometimes be spotted splashing in burns that lead to the north shore. The name of the nearby croft, *Lagandorain*, means 'hollow of the otter'.

hillock to the west is a walled enclosure that was their garden, known to grow excellent vegetables in the sandy soil.

On the seaward side of the same hillock is the former township fank; cobbles, concrete, iron bedsteads, oil drums and driftwood were all combined ingeniously with curves and clefts in the rock. Here the East End crofters would gather for the communal task of dipping and clipping their sheep.

Just before the western boundary gate, which leads into the common grazing and the rougher hill ground, is **Cnoc nam Buachaillean** (hill of the herd-boys). The name is a reminder of human activity from a past era as, from here, the young lads will have watched the cattle on the hill pasture and kept them away from the crops once growing all around.

Croft house at Cnoc Cùil Phàil. From here Malcolm Ferguson set out for Glasgow in 1883, to represent the views of the islanders to the Napier Commission, set up to examine the conditions of highland crofters.
More recently, artist F.C.B. Cadell used to rent the cottage in summer and, from the late 1940s, the early Iona Community youth camps took place here.

The East End Hills – Sliabh Meadhonach

Just west of the herd-boys' hillock a modern fence runs from the shore towards Dun I, parallel with an old wall. This boundary was marked on the 1769 map, with arable rigs right up to it. Now, as then, rough open ground stretches west to the Culbhuirg farm fence. On older maps, the whole of this north-west corner was called the **Sliabh Meadhonach** (middle moorland).

The area is criss-crossed with stone dykes, in a pattern now obscure but which must go back to pre-crofting days. For the last two centuries most of it has provided grazing for the East End township. Once all held in common, several portions are now fenced off for allocation to particular crofts.

It is a rugged, often boggy, but invigorating tramp along the coast from Calva until you reach Dun Bhuirg and the smoother turf of the Machair beyond. You pass the impressive storm beach at **Carraig an Daimh** (Ox Rock), with its huge rounded pebbles and spars of driftwood, and then a string of jagged slocs or gullies. **Sloc nam Ball** (tangles gully) suggests a regular harvest of seaweed and a stone ring about 6.5 metres (21 ft) in diameter, on the flat grass above may have been connected to the kelp burning which boomed in the late eighteenth and early nineteenth centuries. The islanders sold the brittle lumps of ash to merchants for industrial uses such as glass- or soap-making.

More likely the circle marks the foundation of a hut, for the practical purpose of shelter or the more ethereal

Pearly light catches the restless waves which eddy in and out of coves along the coast, west of Port Carraig an Daimh (ox rock bay).

85

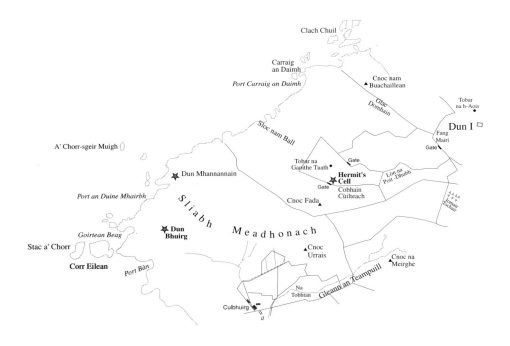

one of contemplation – who knows? People worked out here – rig marks are tucked behind a protective wall above the next gully – and they also milked their cattle in small enclosures of this kind. There again, monks did withdraw to solitary spots for prayer and directly inland from the circle at Sloc nam Ball lies another, more famous one, often called **Hermit's Cell** or Culdee Cell, the latter a mistranslation of the area's name, **Cobhain Cùilteach** (secluded hollow). Round the base of a nearby cliff locals once shifted massive boulders to make a rough fank for penning in cattle or sheep.

There are many who sense a special peace in the atmosphere around this spot and some who find strong spiritual energy in its various stone structures. Belief in the powers of nature is not new, particularly where survival was bound in with the capricious elements. Also close by, under a prominent rock in a dyke, is **Tobar na Gaoithe Tuath** (well of the north wind). The custom was to recite a charm here, to gain a favourable wind for a sea voyage. Malcolm Ferguson, in 1893, was told by a local that there had once been wells for the south, east and west winds also.

A coastal promontory bears an ancient name: **Dun Mhannannain**, Fort of Manann, a Celtic god of the sea. And in Iona last century Alexander Carmichael found lingering knowledge of the ritual of *Diardaoin a' Bhrochain Mhòir* (Thursday of the great porridge) when oatmeal was cast into the sea; the accompanying chant begged for seaweed to enrich the next year's crops.

A few mysteries remain shrouded in names among these hills. It is impossible to know why, at **Fang Mairi**, someone called Mary tilled a patch of walled ground, still glowing green amid the surrounding heather. A wet area below here is recalled in oral tradition as **Lòn na Poit-Dhubh** and, in this case, the translation tells the tale. It was a marsh where the black pot – an illicit still – was hidden, almost certainly from the prying eyes of visiting excisemen!

The Culbhuirg glen was also called **Gleann an Teampuill** (temple glen) but whether this ever had direct religious significance we do not know. Yet at its head, below **Cnoc na Meirghe** (signal rock), there is said to be an early, but now undetectable, burial ground. From the head of the glen a dry-stone dyke reaches east to Cnoc Mòr. This was built by the islanders between 1785 and 1792 on the instructions of the Duke, to create a boundary between the East and the West End Townships.

Stone circle, or hut foundation, in the sheltered hollow called Cobhain Cùilteach.

The Four Roads

For many centuries the prints of feet and hooves made tracks as and where they were needed. In 1848, as part of the public works undertaken in the wake of the potato famine, a road was made from the Sligineach shore across to the Machair. At one point it crossed two farm roads, one leading to Ruanaich and the other to Maol. From this crossroads has come the long-established local term, 'the four roads'. Later last century the circle was completed when a road from the village along the shoreline was created.

Set into the corner wall of the first house above the jetty is a row of horseshoes. Beside here stood the island's main smiddy, in use until horses finally gave way to tractors in the 1950s. It also acted as a store for cargo and was a great meeting-place, to shelter while waiting for the steamer or to exchange stories and news.

Iona folk were known for the training and breeding of horses; indeed their community nickname in Gaelic was *na h-eich* (the horses). Swimming horses across to Mull, to walk them to market, required particular skill. Dugald MacArthur, born in 1910, well remembers the animals being led zig-zag through the shallows until they were waterborne: 'The man in the stern of the boat, the owner, always had the halter and talked to the horse and kept it close up. Then it would swim quite confidently as long as it was within arm's reach of its owner. It would swim quite fast too. At the other end someone jumped out on to the beach and led the horse up. It was always galloped up and down a bit to get the water off.'

A few steps beyond the Martyrs' Bay Restaurant and Finlay Ross's general store is the **War Memorial**, unveiled in 1921 after a series of local fundraising events, including a song recital by Marjory and Patuffa Kennedy-Fraser.

The island's green belt, from the Sligineach shore (foot of picture) across to the Machair. The patchwork of fields, dotted by hillocks, still bear clearly the marks of spade and plough over many centuries. This whole area was worked intensively under the old runrig, or annual lotting, system and then, in the early 19th century, divided up into crofts.

89

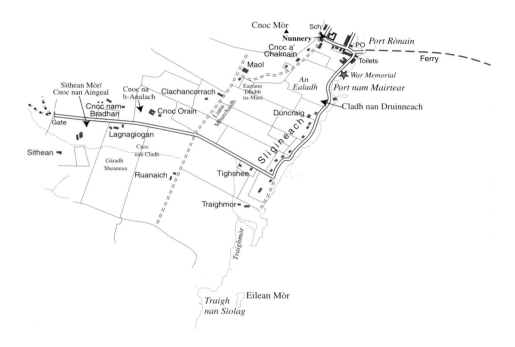

A Remembrance Day service is held here each November.

The attractive curve of sand where the memorial stands has witnessed many scenes in Iona's long history. The Gaelic name **Port nam Mairtear** is obscure. It is popularly linked to the martyrdom of early monks but there is no definite record of any massacre on this spot. Some scholars think it more likely to derive from an old Irish word for remains or relics. In 1853 a writer for the *Ulster Journal of Archaeology* heard it described locally as 'Port nam Marbh' (bay of the dead). The English name now is **Martyrs' Bay**.

The place was certainly long associated with the ritual of death. Here were landed the coffins of kings and chiefs, to be rested first on **An Ealadh**, a grassy mound at the head of the bay and equivalent to an Irish word for 'bier', before being carried along the Street of the Dead to the Reilig Odhráin. Even up to last century this tradition was maintained by funeral parties arriving on the island; the bearers would rest by the mound to take a refreshment before continuing to the graveyard.

The *ealadh* is now at the foot of a farmed field where the soil has yielded further clues that this was an area of some significance. Human bones, most of them from adult females, were discovered there in the 1950s. Cemeteries for different purposes were customary in early medieval times and so this may have been one set apart for women, perhaps before the Nunnery was built.

Slightly further to the south is the site of **Cladh nan Druinneach** (still walled in at the time of Pennant's visit in 1772). This is unlikely to have anything to do with druids, a romantic notion dating from the late eighteenth century. Rather it means the burial ground of the craftsmen, very possibly those skilled sculptors in stone for whom Iona was renowned.

For almost exactly a century up until the early 1980s, the coal puffer beached herself every year at Martyrs Bay. Children streamed excitedly down to watch the procession of carts, and later trailers, load up with what was the main household fuel. Iona had only one small peat moss, the waterlogged area south-east of Dun I, and until 1882 the islanders

Peaceful scene at Sandeels' Bay.

were granted rights to dig peat in the Ross of Mull, transporting it laboriously back over the Sound.

Perched on the rocks south of the bay is a former church, now converted to a private dwelling. This was built as a Free Church in 1849, becoming the United Free Church in 1900 and eventually falling into disuse after that congregation reunited with the Church of Scotland in 1929. Between 1935 and 1939 it was the first home for Dr I. F. Grant's pioneering folk-life collection of tools and artefacts, now on permanent display at the Highland Folk Museum in Kingussie.

Duncraig, which was built to serve as the Free Church Manse in 1894, was bought in 1982 by the American-based Cornerstone Foundation and is run as a quiet holiday house for a small number of guests.

Sligineach (shelly strand) is very descriptive of the shoreline along this road, its sandy indents often strewn thickly with shells. The fields to landward were laid out at the start of the crofting era and still form part of the West End township. A wall runs down beside Duncraig. Dating from about the middle of last century, the building of the wall is remembered as the last example of *mòrlanachd*, the exaction of labour without pay as a tenant's obligation to the Estate. Though the product of a much disliked practice, it is nonetheless a good example of the dry-stone craft.

Where the road turns at right angles away from the sea you can continue to skirt the coast along the track to the croft gate at **Traighmòr** and the big beach, the name's literal meaning, beyond. The broad grassy plain here was a favourite place for the children's sports and picnic organised annually between the wars by some of the regular visitors. The children marched from the village in procession, waving flags.

An easy clamber over the back of the bay brings you down to one of the island's most secluded and lovely beaches, **Traigh nan Sìolag** (Sandeels Bay). When two families at least lived at Traighmòr early last century, all the good ground above Sandeels will have been brought

Looking from Sgurr Mor (big peak), north to Dun I in the distance. The point where the track past Ruanaich house, in the foreground, meets the road was once a regular meeting-place for crofters of the West End township.

under the plough. The late Calum Cameron knew of two unmapped field-names implying that *lìn* or flax was grown around here too – Srath na Lìn and Caol Lìn. We know from documents that there were at least two attempts in the eighteenth century to keep Iona tenants employed spinning flax for linen, but neither experiment was long-lived.

From the Sligineach corner the road runs in a straight line to the crossroads where the right-hand branch, not a public road but maintained by Maol farm as a right of way, goes full circle back to the village. Near the foot of the Maol brae is a seat presented by the Mull and Iona Association to mark their centenary in 1966. Meeting together to share a love of home, and providing mutual assistance, were the aims of several such bodies formed in Glasgow last century by migrants from all over the Highlands and Islands.

Just at the gate below Cnoc Mòr stand the hall and library, two institutions central to rural community life

and both much used. The library was built in 1904 with the help of a grant from Andrew Carnegie, whose parish minister in Sutherland, Robert L. Ritchie, was, fortuitously, from Iona. The hall was opened in 1927 after years of enthusiastic fundraising by locals and visitors alike.

The green hillock where beliefs old and new mingle. It is both the fairy mound, Sithean Mòr, and the hill of angels, Cnoc nan Aingeal.

Also near the foot of the brae, a small Roman Catholic guest-house was built in 1996 by a private charitable body, the Colmcille Trust. They have named it **Cnoc a' Chalmain** (hill of the dove) and visitors are welcome to share in prayer and worship in the little oratory.

Back at the Four Roads, the main road leads straight on to the Machair gate. About half way along, a small hill on the right bears an odd name, **Cnoc na h-Analach** (hill of the breathing) – or so it seems unless you know the story. A young girl was searching for a lost sheep near the cliffs south of the Machair when she chanced on an opening which looked straight down into a cave. There was a stranger, killing the stolen beast. He at once gave chase, at fearsome speed, close enough at one point to grasp her headdress. Only when a group of men appeared in the distance did he give up, fleeing the island – some say to Islay – soon after. The girl collapsed at Cnoc na h-Analach, gasped out the story and breathed her last.

On the left, just before the gate, is **Sìthean Mòr** (big fairy mound), a spot where faith and folklore have been long entangled. In many parts of the Highlands such smooth, green knolls are linked with tales of the wee folk. Here, for example, two Iona fishermen were once enticed inside by the sound of fairy music. One was protected by the metal fishhook he stuck into the door but the other danced for a year before he could escape.

Several eighteenth century visitors saw traces of a stone circle or cairn on top of the hill and heard about the former custom of racing horses sunwise around it on St Michael's day (29 September). Throughout the Hebrides the feast of Michael, who was patron saint of horses, was celebrated in similar fashion, clearly echoing ancient dedications to the sun. Yet another source, the Ramsay of Ochtertyre manuscripts, suggests that here was lit the fire of Beltane on 1 May, when cattle were driven through the flames to purify them and to welcome in the summer.

Christianity has claimed the mound too, perhaps not unexpectedly if it had such powerful pagan connotations. Columba's heavenly vision, as related by Adomnán, is firmly located 'by its very name...for it is called **Cnoc nan Aingeal**, that is the angels' knoll'. Furthermore, in Adomnán's own time rain fell at last, miraculously, on the monks' parched crops after they took Columba's white tunic to the fields and read aloud from the books the saint had copied at the hill of angels. Both names continue to be used for this serene place of mirth and miracles.

The Machair – A' Mhachair

From Dun Bhuirg, looking south-east across the Machair. At least five families survived from the well-worked land around the Dun until Culbhuirg was let as a single farm to Duncan MacPhail from Mull in 1848.

Striking north-west from the gate at the road-end, it is hard to remain unaware of the centuries of labour on the gently undulating turf under your feet.

An area near the shore is named **Lòn nam Manach** (the meadow of the monks) and several incidents in Adomnán refer to planting and harvesting '*in campulo occidentali*', literally 'on the little western plain'. Here may well have been the setting for the 'great festivity and merrymaking' called the Feast of the Ploughmen when, some time after the austere season of Lent, Columba's

Croft land bordering the Machair, drenched in the oblique evening light.

monks were permitted to gather in the cream of the new crop. This fascinating detail was gleaned by Celtic scholar Thomas Clancy from a ninth century document on monastic custom, 'The Monastery of Tallaght'. Its pages reveal that some of the document's main Irish sources were in direct contact with Diarmait, Abbot of Iona.

Shortly before his death Columba was brought to the Machair on a cart to visit brethren working on a stone wall or enclosure. His pronouncement here against poisonous snakes has, they say, kept the island free of adders ever since.

Through the middle ages the ground would have been ploughed. A dense pattern of rigs covers the whole area on the 1769 map and a note states 'arable, a white sandy soil'. The broad furrows remain, particularly visible in low evening sunlight. Since the formation of the crofts, the Machair has been the common grazing for the West End township.

The broad sweep of sea which crashes on to the shingle at the grassland's verge is called, picturesquely, **Camus Cùl an t-Saimh** (bay at the back of the ocean). The silent 's' in the last word makes it sound like 'taav', a corruption of the Old Norse 'haf' for 'ocean'. This is one of only very few place-names of Norse origin in Iona.

Out here, in the dying hours of the year 1865, a three-masted American schooner drifted helplessly in a ferocious storm, her sails torn to ribbons after a stormy crossing from New York. The *Guy Mannering* had been bound for Liverpool with a cargo of cotton and grain. But 15 of her sailors and passengers lost their lives when she foundered on a single rock a mere 400 metres (a quarter of a mile) from the Machair shore. Nineteen, however, were saved owing to the courage of the Iona men who formed a human chain as far into the breakers as they dared. The last to be pulled ashore was Captain Brown and the skerry where white foam still breaks in the middle of the bay has ever since been named Brown's Rock.

Continuing north along the shore takes the walker to one of Iona's most beautiful beaches, **Port Bàn** (fair bay). An earlier name for it was **Port a' Mhurain** (bay of the bent grass). The shelter provided by outlying rocks on either side makes it popular for swimmers.

North of Port Bàn, the commanding position of **Dun Bhuirg** means that its name holds no surprise; literally, this is the hill fort of the fortress. Its steep, knobbly sides come up to a flattish summit which overlooks the western coastline and where part of the defensive wall is still visible. Around a central hearth sheltered Iron Age dwellers, from about 100 BC to AD 200 according to the best archaeological estimate. Excavation has yielded evidence of at least two huts along with indications that the occupants lived from cattle, deer, pig, sheep and seal, used pottery and clay vessels; and one of them had or wore tiny yellow glass beads.

Bordering the sea just to the north is **Goirtean Beag** (little cornfield), where the criss-cross of rig-marks is strikingly obvious from the top of the dun. The whole

area has been intensively cultivated over the years.
During the first half of last century five or six families
crofted the ground now within a single farm, Culbhuirg.

17th hole on the Machair golf course.

Walkers over the Machair may encounter not only
cattle and sheep but, more unexpectedly, the fluttering
flag of a golf pin. In June 1886 Neil MacKay, Iona
correspondent of the *North British Daily Mail*, reported:
'Golf-playing has been introduced into the island by some
English gentlemen who are staying at the Columba
Hotel. The links on the Machair are admirably adapted
for this fashionable sport'.

The first nine-hole course was later extended to 18
and the game became hugely popular with locals and
visitors alike. By the 1920s there was keen competition
for a monthly medal and the whole island would turn out
for a golf match on New Year's Day. In 1968 the
Honourable Company of Iona Golfers, founded by regular
visitors to the Argyll Hotel, revived the idea of an annual
tournament. This cheerful event takes place each August,
raising funds for a local cause.

A sporting fixture to bring in the New Year is an old Highland custom. In Iona football was the precursor of the golf and before that it was a shinty match. This Scottish equivalent of hurling, played with stick and ball and fierce energy, is an ancient pastime, featuring in the tales of early heroes, and the first settlers from Ireland may well have brought it with them to Scotland. Indeed, one of the medieval reworkings of the Columban legend places a quarrel at a hurling match at the heart of events which allegedly drove the monk out of Ireland.

The New Year's shinty was a tremendous day. At the south end of the Machair, just above Port Clacha Geal, is a flat expanse remarkably reminiscent of a sports pitch. All the island's men and boys flocked here in January 1881 for what turned out to be the last such occasion on Iona. Many *camans* – the clubs made of hazel wood from Mull – were smashed into splinters hours later, as the ferocious tussle finally ended in a one-all draw. For eight-year-old Coll MacDonald the spectacle lived on vividly in his memory, to be recalled later in life as a combat of 'Homeric' proportions and a day of joyous excitement.

Bright yellow Bird's-foot-trefoil flourishes in summer, hugging the sandy turf of the Machair.

The West End Hills – Sliabh Siar

At the south end of the Machair the hills rise to form a continuation of the grazing area for the West End crofting township. The old name was **Sliabh Siar** (western moorland). A rough track leads to **Loch Staonaig**, the island's only sizeable expanse of fresh water, which has served as the public reservoir since 1959. The principal source is now scheduled to come from Loch Assapoll in Mull, piped under the Sound to a balancing tank on the slopes of Dun I, but the works at Staonaig continue to be maintained as a back-up should faults occur in the new supply.

A solidly built wall runs from either side of the Loch to the coast. Heather and moss have all but obscured many of its stones but the **Gàradh Dubh Staonaig** (black dyke of the inclining ground) was once a significant boundary, marking off lands to its south as belonging to the medieval Nunnery. The nuns' servants will have milked their cattle out here, enclosing them perhaps in one of the areas still mapped as 'buaile' (fold). Up until the present century, young girls from the West End crofts used to go up to the small shieling huts south of the Loch to do the same, often before going to school.

Near to the Buaile Staonaig, whose walls can still be traced, are several more enclosures and house foundations while to the south lies a flat area with clear signs of tillage. By the eighteenth century Staonaig formed part of a tack, or leased farm, and the most substantial ruin, **John**

Pebbles of every hue, including the prized green serpentine, roll in with each tide at Port an Fhir-Bhreige (bay of the false man) next to Columba's Bay, at the southern tip of the island.

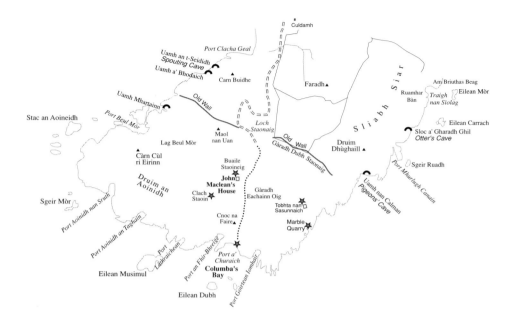

Maclean's House, bears the name of one who held that lease from 1738 to 1757. According to a petition from him, which survives in the Argyll Estate papers, he was very industrious during this period. He repaired the Staonaig enclosure and house, drained the marshy area below Dun I to extract peat and began a short experiment in flax spinning. Maclean spent three months in a London prison in 1747, however, for piloting a store ship to Barra in the Jacobite uprising. He gave himself up at Inveraray, having first evaded arrest on Iona by hiding in the house and then in a cave somewhere in the West End hills.

Just east of John Maclean's House is another walled area, **Gàradh Eachainn Oig** (enclosure of young Hector) whose name, William Reeves was informed in 1857, refers to a Hector Maclean of Duart. This would take us back to the mid-sixteenth century and the period when that family owned Iona.

Other signs of human activity dot the landscape at this southern tip of the island. Sunk into the heathery slope south-west of John Maclean's House is a stone ring commensurate with the dimensions of a prehistoric hut circle. Near here, to the east and past the landmark of Clach Staoin – a large pointed boulder balanced, apparently precariously, on a smaller one – is a hut foundation, about four metres by three (13 ft by 10 ft), with an open entrance. Due south of this is an inlet called **Port Làthraichean** (bay of the ruins). Such ruins as are still visible on the raised-beach above the shore here comprise a rectangular foundation, one wall running from the cliff-face and another making a circular enclosure against it, plus several piles of cleared stones.

It is hard to say when any of the ruins in this whole area south of Loch Staonaig were first occupied. Their most probable recent use was for herds during the centuries when cattle were the main livestock and brought out here for summer grazing. Whoever sowed and harvested the small arable area below John Maclean's House may also have lived in this settlement for a time. **Cnoc na Faire** (look-out knoll) is so called because from its top the herdsmen could watch out for cows trying to browse the growing crops round about.

Looking down to Port a' Churaich, where Columba is said to have landed, from the ruins of John Maclean's House. Signs of cultivation, centuries old, are all around.

The broad expanse of shingle below Cnoc na Faire has long been the focus of pilgrims to Iona as the traditional landing place of Columba and his first companions. Neither Adomnán nor early medieval sources mention any such precise location but, at some stage, the left-hand side of the bay as you face the sea became known as **Port a' Churaich** (port of the coracle). The right-hand side bears the intriguing name of **Port an Fhir-Bhreige** (port of the false man). Up on **Druim an Aoinidh** (ridge of the cliff) to the west is **Càrn Cùl ri Eirinn** (cairn of the back to Ireland) and this too has become woven into the Columban myth, although neither a cairn on this spot nor any story about the saint climbing here on arrival are recorded by visitors prior to the late eighteenth century. Identical place-names are found on Oronsay and Mull and they may have been indicators of boundaries between the lands of the settlers from Ireland and the territories of the Picts.

All around the south coast can be found slivers of

The double expanse of shingle where, it has long been believed, Columba landed in AD 563. The name of the farther inlet, Port a' Churaich (bay of the coracle), commemorates this tradition.

translucent green serpentine but, understandably enough, the bay linked most strongly with Columba has become the most popular spot to scrabble for these coveted souvenirs. The pebbles are considered lucky. Indeed, Keddie's guide-book of 1850 described them as 'anti-magical, medicinal and a preservative against shipwreck'.

Other Columban associations have coloured the interpretation of various landscape features round about. A grassy mound about 20 metres (65 ft) long at the head of the bay looks a little like an upturned coracle. Early travellers' accounts enthusiastically embrace the notion that this must have been where the saint buried his boat upon arrival. The local view, more aware of the rigours of island life, has more often been that sea transport was the last thing any new settler would get rid of. Excavation at the end of last century found no evidence that the mound is man-made and it is probably a remnant from the raised beach.

The origin of around 50 pebble cairns directly above Port an Fhir-Bhreige is less clear, however. Most are quite small, between 1 and 3 metres (3 and 10 ft) in diameter but two reach nearly 6 metres (20 ft) across and are over 1.5 metres (4 ft 9 in) high. They have not been excavated to date. To pile a few stones together, and to add a stone thereafter, is a common and long-established act of remembrance or devotion. The cairns were perhaps created and maintained by monks and pilgrims centuries ago. One belief was that they were a form of penance, provoking Pennant's wry observation that among the brothers there must have been some 'enormous sinners'.

The coasts of the south end afford good walks but care should always be taken as the cliffs, although not spectacularly high, can be steep and rocky and are split by deep ravines.

Just above where the rocks begin to rise from the Machair shore is the island's best known natural phenomenon, **Uamh an t-Seididh** or **Spouting Cave**. At half-tide and when there is a good swell, water surging into the sea-level aperture hits the end of the rocky

passage and is forced up through a chimney-like fissure in
its roof. The immediate area can therefore be slippery and
should be approached with caution. Walking south over
the Machair you might well hear the boom of the
frustrated wave and see the plume of spray shooting
skywards.

Very close by is **Uamh a' Bhodaich** (the old man's
cave), now not much more than a grassy ledge against the
seaward cliff-face. It is linked with the story of Cnoc na
h-Analach (see Chapter 8), as the spot where the sheep-
stealer was said to be hiding.

About 500 metres (550 yds) along, set into the side
of a pebble-filled gully which fills up at high tide, is a
neat little cave called **Uamh Mhartainn**, (usually
translated as St Martin's Cave). St Martin of Tours was
highly regarded in the early Irish church. His name
appeared in the liturgy of the Columban monks and one
of the high crosses of Iona was dedicated to him. On the
other hand the cave might simply have been associated,
for reasons unknown, with someone called Martin.

Pigeons' Cave. Its lower
and upper levels are
home to the rock dove.

Port Beul Mòr takes a large bite out
of the south-west corner of the island,
attesting to the meaning of its name, 'bay of
the big mouth'. Boats used to be kept here,
ready to set out westwards after big fish such
as cod. The late Calum Cameron recalled
his father talking of these marathon
expeditions when he had been a boy:
'...they never took food, just water...it was
an awful long day. He said they would be so
tired walking back from Beul Mòr with the
fish'. It may be that fishing tackle was kept
in the oblong pit at the head of the bay.
Measuring about 1.35 by 2.60 metres (4.5 by
8.6 ft) and 60 centimetres (23 in) deep, this
has been well made and is lined with the
beach's large round pebbles, but its original
purpose is unclear.

Along the south-east coast are a couple

Stone-lined pit at the head of the big storm beach at Port Beul Mòr, a bay once used regularly by local fisherman.

more caves of interest. Just south of Sandeels Bay is **Sloc a' Gharadh Ghil** (gully of the white den), but whose alternative English name is **Otters' Cave**. It is a slit in the rock-face which can really only safely be seen from the sea but otters are occasionally spied swimming after fish in the vicinity. **Uamh nan Calman (Pigeons' Cave)**, about 500 metres (550 yds) to the south, was a favourite haunt of Henry D. Graham in the early 1850s, where he collected eggs, sketched and shot birds. Although he noted that the island had 'as many as nine or ten caves frequented by pigeons' this double cleft in the cliff, right by the sea, was a particularly good nesting place for the rock doves. A jumble of huge boulders block the steep gully leading down to the cave, but they have formed a low tunnel allowing access through to the shore.

Tucked into the rugged coastline of Iona's south-east corner lies an unusual site for a Hebridean island, the **Marble Quarry**. It is not advisable to try reaching it directly along the shore, as this is very indented and impassable in places. The simplest route is to follow the broad, green valley that runs toward the sea from the ruins above Port a' Churaich. A sign that you are on the right track is when the remains of two buildings come into view. That on the left has been known by two names locally, **Tobhta nan Sasunnaich** (ruin of the lowlanders or English-speakers) and **Tigh nan Gall** (house of the strangers or lowlanders). Both indicate the probable origin of this long rectangle of dry-stone walls, its corners rounded in the style typical of an eighteenth-century dwelling with thatched roof and central hearth.

Here, around 1790, lived quarrymen imported with their specialist skills from mainland Scotland or perhaps

even England. Their language would certainly have set them apart from the local population at that time, none of whom, except the schoolmaster, would have had more than a word or two of English. Did the new residents fraternise nonetheless? We don't know, but older folk used to say that the strains of the pipes in this isolated spot could be heard on the wind long after Tigh nan Gall fell into ruins.

It was a bold but short-lived experiment by the Duke of Argyll. Spurred by the enthusiasm of his adviser, German geologist Rudolph Raspe, for a potential 'new Scotch Carrara', the plan was to market marble from Iona and Tiree in the fashionable cities of Europe. The seam had been quarried intermittently for local use earlier than this; the altar table in the medieval Abbey church, for example, was reputed to be of Iona marble. The difficulty of extraction and transport on any viable scale, however, put paid to the 1790 scheme. Not until 1907 was there another attempt and the concrete foundations to the

From the high ground just above the south end of the Machair, the Sliabh Siar (above) – western moorland – stretches in uneven dips and hummocks to the coast. The Paps of Jura, some 30 miles (50 km) to the south-east, appear to float above the sea mist.

Looking north from the same spot, along the broad sweep of the Bay at the Back of the Ocean (right). A day which shows off the brilliant colours and clear light for which Iona is famed.

right as you descend are those of a workmen's hut erected during this second, more successful commercial venture.

Veer right past the second hut and you reach the top of a narrow gully which leads down into the quarry itself. A large cast-iron skeleton, a cutting frame, is silhouetted against the white blocks piled higgledy-piggledy behind. Clambering down you pass a stone water tank, a sturdy gas engine and two supply tanks. The remains of a bogie, or wheeled platform, lies at an angle among the rubble.

In 1972 a thorough survey of the quarry was carried out by a small team of archaeologists one of whom, David Viner, has published the findings in booklet form. It is a fascinating story. The attractive, green-veined stone was in demand in the early years of this century for wall-facings, wash-stands, altars, pulpits and fonts and for a variety of popular souvenirs and ornaments. There must have been noise, heat and bustle then, as coke burned furiously in the gas generator tank, the saws whirred and men worked two huge derricks – now long gone – to swing the cut blocks to a waiting puffer. At low tide you can climb more easily over to where mooring rings are still visible in the outcrop of rock that served as a rough jetty. Below you might catch a glimpse of gleaming cargo which never made it aboard in these frequently choppy waters.

There was work for a few local men during this phase of the quarry's life, but the outbreak of war in 1914 dealt a severe blow. Men left to join up, the lucrative trade with Belgium ceased and by 1919 the company was bankrupt and wound up its operations.

Such is the rarity of pre-First World War industrial remains of this kind *in situ* that the quarry machinery has been listed as a Scheduled Ancient Monument. As with all such designations, it is thus an offence to damage or remove anything from the site. The National Trust for Scotland, in consultation with Historic Scotland, is carrying out a programme of preservation and maintenance, to stem further corrosion of the equipment and to ensure that it remains in a safe condition.

From the quarry, walkers may return to the loch and the track down to the Machair, or they can strike out parallel to the south-east coastline, across the high stretch of moorland called **Druim Dhùghaill** (Dugald's Ridge). An old tale has it that a lad named Dugald was killed here by a fairy woman, when he went to hunt rabbits and forgot to take with him the steel arrow which a blacksmith had forged for his protection. It seems a bleak place indeed but there are signs of real human labour too in the rigmarks snaking across the ridge. These were worked by crofters from the West End, probably when the population was at its height in the middle of last century and every possible strip was brought under the plough.

Eventually the moor drops down to the short township track leading by Ruanaich house to the centre of the Four Roads.

Ruins of a cottage built to house workers at the marble quarry in the 1970s. In the distance lies the southern tip of the Ross of Mull.

Islets

Iona's coast is strewn with rocks, skerries and small islands. Several of these have long been bound into the local economy as good fishing water or, at one time, as hunting grounds for seals or sea-fowl and their eggs or as extra grazing.

The largest is **Soa** (sheep island), lying three kilometres (two miles) south-west of Iona. It was allocated jointly to the West End crofters and, up until the 1960s, 20-30 ewes were regularly taken out in the spring and left until the autumn. The men went back out later to clip the wool for sending off in July. Although the approach by sea is steep and rugged, there is good grass and sorrel is also said to grow there.

Henry D. Graham made regular trips to Soa in the early 1850s in search of its rich bird life. He described it as high and rocky, with grassy banks about 24 metres (80 ft) above sea-level which fed a dozen sheep, and burrowed into its soft, deep soil he found the 'minute galleries' where the Stormy Petrel nested.

According to Adomnán, the Columban monks took seals, useful for their meat, skins and oil, from a small nearby island where they bred. This may well have been Soa, although Erraid off the south end of the Ross of Mull is another possibility.

Eilean Musimul (mouse island) and **Eilean na h-Aon Chaorach** (one-sheep island), close to the south coast, went with the croft just south of the village which, early last century, was worked by the innkeeper at Iona Cottage. By the 1850s this holding was amalgamated into Maol farm. A few sheep were probably put out to these two islets at one time although the latter, as its name suggests, may only ever have had enough grass for a single sheep.

The outline of Soa (sheep island), from the Ross of Mull, in the glow of a winter sunset.

115

Eilean Chalbha (calf island) lies very near to the north shore and signifies a small island off a larger one. Of Norse origin, the name became transferred as 'Calva' across to the two crofting holdings opposite, to which it belongs. Sheep were last grazed here about 20 years ago. Gulls once nested on the islet's crags but recent ravages by mink have all but put an end to that.

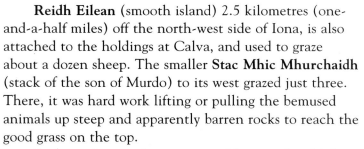

Seals frequent several of Iona's outlying islets, basking on the rocks or popping a curious head above water to survey passing craft.

Reidh Eilean (smooth island) 2.5 kilometres (one-and-a-half miles) off the north-west side of Iona, is also attached to the holdings at Calva, and used to graze about a dozen sheep. The smaller **Stac Mhic Mhurchaidh** (stack of the son of Murdo) to its west grazed just three. There, it was hard work lifting or pulling the bemused animals up steep and apparently barren rocks to reach the good grass on the top.

Seals are frequently seen around here and seabirds are numerous. Dugald MacArthur remembers collecting gulls' eggs, for preserving or for use in baking, at Reidh Eilean and Eilean Chalbha after taking out sheep to these islands.

Eilean Annraidh (storm island), off the north-east tip of Iona, has featured in countless paintings and photographs of the famous 'white strand of the monks' opposite. On a fine summer's day, its own slender spit of sand across the turquoise water lacks only a palm tree to conjure up, for a moment, images of a tropical island.

Although allocated to the croft at Boineach, now

called Bishop's Walk, it has not been used for grazing within memory. The island is said to be prone to rats and marram grass may also have encroached too heavily on what grass cover there is. Once a haven for nesting terns, it is also unfortunately now the home of mink which are undoubtedly responsible for eliminating these bird colonies. From the back of Eilean Annraidh across to Eilean Chalbha was known as a good place to run a line for mackerel or for big fish such as cod and lythe.

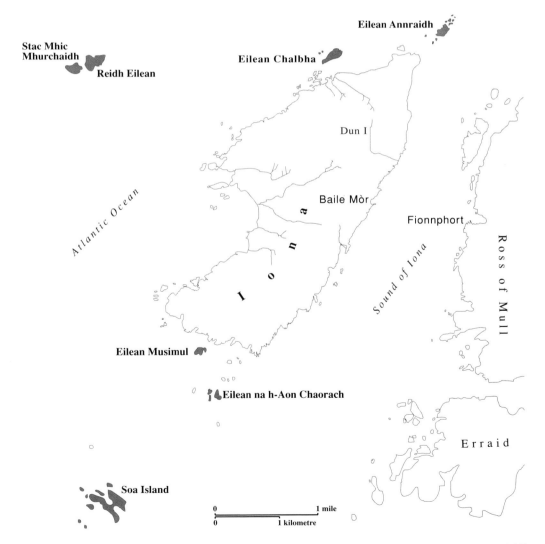

Eilean Annraidh

Stac Mhic Mhurchaidh

Eilean Chalbha

Reidh Eilean

Dun I

Atlantic Ocean

Baile Mòr

Fionnphort

I o n a

Sound of Iona

Ross of Mull

Eilean Musimul

Eilean na h-Aon Chaorach

Erraid

Soa Island

0   1 mile
0   1 kilometre

Grey rock and grassy turf, salt breezes and the swirl of white water –
the look of Hebridean landscape is often fresh and raw, the feel of it enduring.
For many, Iona is a special place, reflecting eternal values. In an old Gaelic saying, both
Ireland and grey-green Islay may sink below a great tide before the day of judgement.
But the island of Columba the churchman will swim above the waves.
Ach snàmhaidh I Choluim Chlèirich.

Chronology

BC

c. 3500 Occasional occupation by Stone Age farmers.

c. 2000 Possible Bronze Age burial cairn.

c. 100 Occupation of Dun Bhuirg by Iron Age settlers.

AD

563 Arrival of Columba from Ireland; founding of monastic settlement on Iona soon after.

574 Ordination by Columba of Aedán as king of Dál Riata.

597 Death of Columba.

634 Monastery at Lindisfarne founded by monk from Iona.

664 Synod of Whitby.

679 Adomnàn succeeds as Abbot of Iona.

795 First Viking raid on Iona.

c. 800 Carving of the high crosses.

802 Burning of monastery by Vikings.

806 Third Viking attack and slaughter of 68 monks.

807-14 Abbot Cellach builds new Columban house at Kells.

825 Attack by raiders but Columba's shrine saved.

849 Relics of Columba divided between Kells and Dunkeld.

858 Death of Kenneth MacAlpin; annals claim he was buried in Iona.

986 Slaughter of abbot and 15 monks by unidentified Norsemen.

1097 Donald Bane, son of King Duncan, died and buried at Dunkeld; but annals claim his bones subsequently removed to Iona.

1098 Expedition by Magnus Barelegs, King of Norway; respect for a chapel on Iona recorded in the saga.

1099 Names of abbots of Iona still mentioned in Annals of Ulster.

c.1180 Building of St Oran's Chapel, possibly for the MacDonald Lords of the Isles.

c. 1200 Founding of Benedictine Abbey and Nunnery by Reginald, son of Somerled.

c. 1200 Building of parish church of St Ronan.

1203 Papal bull mentions founding of new Monastery on Iona.

1372 Papal records mention rector for parish of St Ronan on Iona.

1380 John, Lord of the Isles, buried on Iona.

1421 Abbot Dominic MacKenzie succeeds; oversees extensive rebuilding, including replacement of two-level choir, broadening of nave and construction of the tower.

1499 Bishopric of the Isles and Abbacy of Iona brought together; the Abbey church acts de facto as Cathedral of the Isles.

1549 Tour of islands by Donald Monro Dean of the Isles; earliest extant description of Iona by visitor.

1574 Last Prioress of Iona, Marion Maclean, gives up Nunnery lands in favour of Hector Maclean of Duart.

1609 Statutes of Iona.

1675 List of heads of household in Iona (24 names).

1688 William Sacheverell, Governor of Man, visits Iona.

1690s Campbells of Argyll gain supremacy over Maclean territory in Mull and Iona.

1693 Description of Iona collected by Sir Robert Sibbald; later published in MacFarlane's Geographical Collections.

1695 Martin Martin visits Iona.

1738-57 John Maclean tacksman of East End.

1755 Petition to Duke of Argyll from West End tenants, Iona.

1764 Revd Dr John Walker visits for his Report on the Hebrides.

1769 Estate map of Iona drawn by William Douglas.

1772 Thomas Pennant visits Iona; the account of his Scottish tour incorporates Sir Joseph Banks' description of Staffa, the first ever published.

1773 Dr Samuel Johnson and James Boswell visit Iona.

1774 First schoolmaster appointed on Iona, by the SSPCK.

1779 List of inhabitants on the Argyll Estate drawn up for 5th Duke; in Iona were 32 tenants and 12 cottars, total population 249.

1790 The Marble Company working the marble quarry.

1792-94	Flax-spinning trial.		Machair shore.
1792	Completion of dyke dividing East and West Ends.	1866	Mull and Iona Association formed in Glasgow.
1802-04	Crofts laid out and allocated to 30 tenants.	1867	Cottage in village built up to become Argyll Hotel.
1804	Old Parochial Register begun for Iona, recording marriages and baptisms.	1868	First Free Church manse converted to become St Columba Hotel.
1818	John Keats visits Iona.	1870	Stone known as St Columba's Pillow unearthed.
1820	Visit of Revd Legh Richmond who donates first library books.	1871	Population 236 at Census.
1822	Paddle-steamer the *Comet* sails from Fort William to Staffa and Iona.	1874-76	Consolidation of Abbey ruins under Rowand Anderson.
1828	Parish Church and Manse built, to Thomas Telford design	1878	The Duchess's Cross erected, to first wife of 8th Duke of Argyll.
1835	Record of deaths begun in Old Parochial Register.	1881	Population 243 at Census.
1835	Royal Commission on Religious Instruction, Scotland records highest documented population total for Iona, 521.	1881	Last New Year's Day shinty match held on the Machair.
		1882	End of peat-cutting rights on Mull, start of coal puffer service.
1841	First nominal national Census, 496 on Iona.	1883	Napier Commission inquiry into conditions of crofters in the Highlands & Islands; Iona evidence given by Malcolm Ferguson, Cnoc Cul Phail.
1843	Disruption of the Church of Scotland; Iona minister Revd Donald McVean comes out to form Free Church congregation.	1885	Presentation of bookcase and books to islanders by Thomas Cook (now on display in Iona Heritage Centre).
1846	First year of the potato famine.	1886	Golf-course laid out on the Machair.
1847	Rents raised 50% in Iona; start of Estate-assisted emigration, mostly to North America, and at least 100 leave the island.	1890	New Crofters' Commission held hearings in Bunessan and Iona; all rents reduced.
		1891	Population 247 at Census.
1847	Royal cruise of Hebrides; Prince Albert lands on Iona, but Queen Victoria remains on board.	1894	Episcopal retreat house and chapel built.
1848	Public road built from Sligineach shore to Machair.	1897	Commemorative services in Gaelic and English for 1300th anniversary of St Columba's death.
1848	Letting of first farm, Culbhuirg, formed from 5-6 former crofts to Duncan MacPhail of Torosay in Mull.	1897	Opening of new Post Office on village brae; telegraph begins.
1849	*Barlow* sails for Canada from Greenock; 52 Iona people on board.	1897	Cairn built on Dun I to mark Diamond Jubilee of Queen Victoria.
1850	First proper slipway built at Port Rònain, part of public works programme following potato famine.	1899	Gift of ecclesiastical ruins to new Iona Cathedral Trust by 8th Duke of Argyll.
1851	Population 337 at Census.	1900	Death of 8th Duke of Argyll.
1851	Receiving house for mail set up in village with Archibald MacDonald as first postmaster.	1901	Population 213 at Census.
		1904	Public library built with funds from Andrew Carnegie and opened by Lady Victoria Campbell.
1852	*Marmion* sails for Australia from Liverpool; 31 Iona people on board, assisted by the Highland & Island Emigration Society.	1905	Restored choir and transepts of Abbey church opened.
		1907-14	Marble Quarry in operation.
1858	Graveslabs in Reilig Odhràin rearranged into two ridges.	1909	First wedding in restored Abbey church, Archibald MacArthur to Janet MacNiven.
1861	Population 263 at Census.	1910	Restored nave of Abbey church opened.
1865	*Guy Mannering* shipwrecked off	1911	Population 222 at Census.

1912	Marble effigies of Duke and Duchess of Argyll installed in Abbey church.	1965	Rebuilding of Abbey west range, completing restoration.
1914-18	World War I; Iona part of a restricted area.	1967	Revd George MacLeod created a life peer.
1920	Garden established in Nunnery ruins, gift of the J.J. Spencer family.	1968	Honourable Company of Iona Golfers formed.
1921	Population 234 at Census.	1968	Visit by Queen Elizabeth the Queen Mother.
1921	War Memorial unveiled.		
1922	Catherine MacCormick, widow of James MacArthur, reaches 100th birthday; (died aged 100 years 11 months).	1970	St John's Cross replica erected on original site.
		1971	Population 145 at Census.
		1973	Local inquiry into proposal for Mull-Iona car ferry.
1923	First wireless set on the island.	1974	Last season of *King George V* and of daily steamer trips from Oban to Staffa and Iona.
1927	Village hall opened.		
1929	Retirement of Coll Maclean, last ferryman to use sail on the Fionnphort-Iona run.		
		1979	The Hugh Fraser Foundation buys Iona for the nation; ownership transferred to the National Trust for Scotland.
1931	Population 141 at Census.		
c. 1931	Telephone installed at Post Office.		
1931	New bell installed in Abbey belfry, gifted by visitor D.G. Dunn.	1979	First car ferry service, with MV *Morvern*, between Iona and Fionnphort.
1935-39	*Am Fasgadh* (the Highland Folk Museum) set up in empty United Free Church, Martyrs Bay by Dr I.F. Grant.	1981	Population 103 at Census.
		1984	Mary-Ann Maclean reaches 100th birthday; (died aged 105).
1936	First service to be broadcast from the Cathedral, for Gaelic radio.	1985	Parish of Iona linked with that of Bunessan
1938	Founding of the Iona Community by the Revd George F. MacLeod.	1988	The MacLeod Centre, run by the Iona Community, opens.
1938	First motor vehicle on the island, the Iona Community lorry.	1990	St John's Cross restored and housed in Abbey Museum.
1938-45	World War II; Iona part of a restricted area.	1990	Iona Heritage Centre opens in the manse.
1940	Chapter-house and library restored by Iona Community.	1990	Custom-built doctor's surgery opened for use of medical staff visiting from Mull.
1947	Restored Abbey refectory re-roofed.		
1951	Population 173 at Census.	1991	Population 130 at Census.
1954	Abbey east range restored.	1991	Death of Lord MacLeod of Fuinary, founder of the Iona Community.
1956	Visit by the Queen, the Duke of Edinburgh and Princess Margaret; attended a service in the Abbey church.	1991	New vehicle ferry for Iona, *Loch Buie*, able to carry 250 passengers and 10 cars, launched at St Monans Yard, Fife.
1957	St Oran's Chapel re-roofed.		
1957	Electricity supply switched on at public ceremony in hall.	1993	Start of work to lay new water pipe, supplied from Loch Assapoll in Mull, underneath Sound of Iona.
1959	Jacques Lipchitz sculpture placed in completed cloister garth.	1996	Visit by the Princess Royal during General Assembly week.
1959	Loch Staonaig made into public reservoir.	1996	Work begins to replace cap house on Abbey tower; completed November.
1961	Population 130 at Census.		
1961	Last working horse put out to graze.		
1963	Celebrations to mark 1400th anniversary of Columba's landing.	1996	Roman Catholic house for retreat and worship built.
1964	First car ferry *Columba* begins Oban-Mull service, under Captain Colin MacDonald of Iona.	1997	1400th anniversary of the death of St Columba.

Bird Checklist

These are the resident and migrant birds which may generally be seen, at some season of the year, on Iona or in its surrounding waters. Those marked + are less common and are confined to the species-favoured locality. The Gaelic and Latin names are also listed.

SEA BIRDS

Arctic Skua+ – *Fasgadair/Stercorarius parasiticus*
Arctic Tern – *Stearnal/Sterna paradisaea*
Black Guillemot – *Gerra-breac/Cepphus grylle*
Black-headed Gull – *Faoileag a' chinn duibh/Larus ridibundus*
Common Gull – *Faoileag/Larus canus*
Common Tern – *Stearnag/Sterna hirundo*
Cormorant – *Sgarbh/Phalacrocorax carbo*
Fulmar – *Eun crom/Fulmarus glacialis*
Gannet – *Guga/Sula bassana*
Great Black-backed Gull – *Farspag/Larus marinus*
Great Skua+ – *Fasgadair mor/Stercorarius skua*
Guillemot – *Eun dubh an sgadain/Uria aalge*
Herring Gull – *Faoileag an sgadain/Larus argentatus*
Kittiwake – *Ruideag/Rissa tridactyla*
Lesser Black-backed Gull – *Faoileag bheag/Larus fuscus*
Manx Shearwater+ – *Fachadh ban/Puffinus puffinus*
Puffin+(on Reidh Eilean) – *Buthaid/Fratercula arctica*
Razorbill – *Falc/Alca torda*
Shag – *Sgarbh an sgumain/Phalacrocorax aristotelis*
Storm Petrel+ (on Soa) – *Paraig/Hydrobates pelagicus*

WADERS

Common Sandpiper – *Luatharan/Tringa hypoleucos*
Curlew – *Guilbneach/Numenius arquata*
Dunlin – *Graillig/Calidris alpina*
Golden Plover – *Feadag/Pluvialis apricaria*
Greenshank – *Deoch bhuidhe/Tringa nebularia*
Grey Heron – *Corra ghritheach/Ardea cinerea*
Lapwing – *Carracag/Vanellus vanellus*
Oystercatcher – *Gille brighde/Haematopus ostralegus*
Purple Sandpiper+ – *Luatharan rioghail/Calidris maritima*
Redshank – *Cam-ghlas/Tringa totanus*
Ringed Plover – *Trilleachan traghad/Charadrius hiaticula*
Snipe – *Naosg/Gallinago gallinago*
Turnstone – *Gobhlachan/Arenaria interpres*

DIVERS

Black-throated Diver+ – *Learga dhubh/Gavia arctica*
Great Northern Diver+ – *Muir bhuachaill/Gavia immer*
Red-throated Diver+ – *Learga ruadh/Gavia stellata*

PASSERINE

Blackbird – *Lon dubh/Turdus merula*
Blue Tit – *Cailleachag cheann ghorm/Parus caeruleus*
Chaffinch – *Breacan beithe/Fringilla coelebs*
Coal Tit – *Smutag/Parus ater*
Collared Dove – *Calman a' chrios/Streptopelia decaocto*
Dunnock – *Gealbhonn nam preas/Prunella modularis*
Fieldfare – *Liath thruisg/Turdus pilaris*
Goldcrest – *Crionag bhuidhe/Regulus regulus*

Great Tit – *Currac bhain tighearna/Parus major*
Greenfinch – *Glaisean daraich/Carduelis chloris*
House Martin – *Gobhlan taighe/Delichon urbica*
House Sparrow – *Gealbhonn/Passer domesticus*
Linnet – *Gealan lin/Acanthis cannabina*
Meadow Pipit – *Snathag/Anthus pratensis*
Pied Wagtail – *Breac an t-sil/Motacilla alba*
Redwing – *Sgiath dhearg/Turdus iliacus*
Reed Bunting – *Gealag loin/Emberiza schoeniculus*
Robin – *Bru dhearg/Erithacus rubecula*
Rock Dove+ – *Calman creige/Columba livia*
Rock Pipit – *Gabhagan/Anthus spinoletta*
Sedge Warbler – *Glas eun/Acrocephalus schoenobaenus*
Siskin+ – *Gealag bhuidhe/Carduelis spinus*
Skylark – *Uiseag/Alauda arvensis*
Song Thrush – *Smeorach/Turdus philomelos*
Starling – *Druid/Sturnus vulgaris*
Stonechat – *Clacharan/Saxicola torquata*
Swallow – *Gobhlan gaoithe/Hirundo rustica*
Swift – *Gobhlan mor/apus apus*
Tree Pipit – *Riabhaig/Anthus trivialis*
Twite+ – *Gealan beinne/Acauthis flavirostris*
Wheatear – *Bru gheal/Oenanthe oenanthe*
Whinchat – *Gocan/Saxicola rubetra*
Willow Warbler – *Crionag ghiuthais/ Phylloscopus trochilus*
Wren – *Dreathan donn/Troglodytes troglodytes*
Yellowhammer – *Buidheag bhealaidh/ Emberiza citrinella*

HAWKS
Buzzard – *Clamhan/Buteo buteo*
Hen Harrier+ – *Breid air toin/Circus cyaneus*
Peregrine+ – *Seabhag/Falco peregrinus*
Sparrowhawk – *Speireag/Accipiter nisus*

WILDFOWL
Eider – *Lach lochlannach/Somateria mollissima*
Red-breasted Merganser – *Siolta dhearg/ Mergus serrator*
Shelduck – *Cra-gheadh/Tadorna tadorna*
Corncrake+ – *Traon/Crex crex*
Barnacle Goose+ – *Cathan/Branta leucopsis*
Greylag Goose+ – *Geadh glas/Anser anser*
White-fronted Goose+ – *Geadh bhlar/ Anser albifrons*
Whooper Swan+ – *Eala bhan/Cygnus cygnus*
Common Scoter – *Lach bheag dubh/ Melanitta nigra*

CORVUS
Hooded Crow – *Feannag/Corvus corone*
Jackdaw – *Gathag/Corvus monedula*
Raven – *Fitheach/Corvus corax*
Rook – *Rocas/Corvus frugilegus*

CUCHLIDAE
Cuckoo – *Cuthag/Cuculus canorus*

Birds of passage only include these waders :
Bar-tailed Godwit – *Cearra ghob mhor/ Limosa lapponica*
Grey Plover+ – *Trilleachan/Pluvialis squatarola*
Knot – *Luatharan gainmhich/Calidris canutus*
Sanderling – *Luatharan glas/Calidris alba*

And easterly winds can bring odd **vagrants** to the island, for example the Common Rosefinch in the spring of 1995 and the Waxwing, seen in winter 1996.

Plant Checklist

A comprehensive list of flowering plants, along with rushes, sedges, grasses, and ferns, can be found in *Flowers of Iona* by Jean Millar, published in 1993. This extract of the most common plants is listed by habitat and followed by their Gaelic and botanical names.

ARABLE

Butterbur – *Gallan Mòr/Petasites hybridus*
Corn Marigold – *Bile Bhuidhe/ Chrysanthemum segetum*
Corn-cockle – *Lus Loibheach/ Agrostemma githago*
Corn Spurrey – *Cluain-lìn,Corran-lìn Spergula arvensis*
Cow Parsley – *Costag Fhiadhain/ Anthriscus sylvestris*
Hogweed – *Odharan/Heracleum sphondylium*
Knapweed – *Cnapan Dubh/Centaurea nigra*
Lady's Bedstraw – *Lus an Leasaich Rùin/Galium verum*
Long-headed Poppy – *Crom-lus Fad-cheannach/Papaver dubium*
Oxeye Daisy – *Neòinean Mòr/ Leucanthemum vulgare*
Parsley-piert – *Spionan Moire Caol/ Aphanes inexspectata*
Scarlet Pimpernel – *Falcair/Anagallis arvensis*
Yellow Rattle – *Modhalan Buidhe/ Rhinanthus minor*

SANDY SHORE

Marram Grass – *Muran/Ammophila arenaria*
Ray's Knotgrass – *Glùineach na Tràighe/ Polygonum oxyspermum*
Saltwort – *Lus an t-Salainn/Salsola kali*
Sea Rocket – *Fearsaideag/Cakile maritima*
Sea-holly – *Cuileann Tràgha/Eryngium maritimum*
Sea-milkwort – *Lus na Saillteachd/ Glaux maritima*
Silverweed – *Brisgean/Potentilla anserina*

MACHAIR

Common Bird's-foot-trefoil – *Barra-mhìslean,Peasair a' Mhadaidh-ruaidh/ Lotus corniculatus*
Common Stork's-bill – *Gob Corra/ Erodium cicutarium*
Daisy – *Neòinean/Bellis perennis*
Dove's-foot Crane's-bill – *Crobh Preachain Mìn/Geranium molle*
Milkwort – *Lus a' Bhainne/Polygala vulgaris*
Thyme – *Lus na Machraidh,Lus an Righ/Thymus polytrichus subsp. britannicus*
Wild Carrot – *Curran Talmhainn/ Daucus carota subsp. carota*

HEATH

Bell Heather – *Fraoch a' Bhadain, Biadh na Circe-fraoich/Erica cinerea*
Blaeberry – *Caora-mhitheag/Vaccinium myrtillus*

Cross-leaved Heath – *Fraoch Frangach/ Erica tetralix*

Crowberry – *Lus na Feannaig/ Empetrum nigrum*

Devil's-bit Scabious – *Greim an Diabhail,Ura-bhallach/Succisa pratensis*

Eyebright – *Lus nan Leac/Euphrasia agg*

Heath Spotted-orchid – *Mogairlean Mòintich/Dactylorhiza maculata subsp. ericetorum*

Heather – *Fraoch/Calluna vulgaris*

Mountain Everlasting – *Spòg Cait/ Antennaria dioica*

Juniper – *Iubhar Beinne/Juniperus communis subsp. alpina*

Tormentil – *Cairt Làir/Potentilla erecta*

BOG

Bog Asphodel – *Bliochan/Narthecium ossifragum*

Bog Pimpernel – *Falcair Lèana/ Anagallis tenella*

Bogbean – *Trì-bhileach, Pònair Chapaill/ Menyanthes trifoliata*

Butterwort – *Mòthan/Pinguicula vulgaris*

Lousewort – *Lus Riabhach Monaidh/ Pedicularis palustris*

Marsh Cinquefoil – *Còig-bhileachUisge/ Potentilla palustris*

Marsh Pennywort – *Lus na Peighinn/ Hydrocotyle vulgaris*

Marsh St John's-wort – *Meas an Tuirc-Allta/Hypericum elodes*

Sundew – *Lus na Feàrnaich/Drosera rotundifolia*

ROCK FACE AND GULLIES

Angelica – *Lus nam Buaidh, Aingealag/ Angelica sylvestris*

Bloody Crane's-bill – *Creachlach Dearg/Geranium sanguineum*

Bluebell – *Fuath-mhuc, Bròg na Cuthaig/Hyacinthoides non-scripta*

Burnet Rose – *Ròs Beag Bàn na h-Alba/ Rosa pimpinellifolia*

Dog Violet – *Dail-chuach/Viola riviniana*

Honeysuckle – *Iadh-shlat, Lus na Meala/Lonicera periclymenum*

Lovage – *Sunais/Ligusticum scoticum*

Meadow-rue – *Rù Beag/Thalictrum minus subsp. arenarium*

Primrose – *Sòbhrach/Primula vulgaris*

Ramsons – *Creamh,Gairgean/Allium ursinum*

Roseroot – *Lus nan Laoch/Sedum rosea*

Scurvey-grass – *Carran Albannach/ Cochlearia officinalis subsp. scotica*

Sea Campion – *Coirean na Mara/ Silene uniflora*

Thrift – *Neòinean Cladaich/Armeria maritima*

Wall Pennywort – *Leacan/Umbilicus rupestris*

LEDGES

Common Centuary – *Ceud-bhileach, Deagha Dearg/Centaurium erythraea*

Early-purple Orchid – *Moth-ùrach/ Orchis mascula*

Field Gentian – *Lus a' Chrubain/ Gentianella campestris*

Frog Orchid – *Mogairlean Losgainn/ Coeloglossum viride*

Spring Squill – *Lear-uinnean/Scilla verna*

Bibliography

Anderson, A.O. and Anderson, M.O. *Adomnan's Life of Columba*, Edinburgh 1961, 2nd edn Oxford 1991

Boswell, J. *Journal of a Tour to the Hebrides*, edited by F.A. Pottle and C. H. Bennett, London 1936

British Museum (Natural History), Department of Botany *The Island of Mull, a Survey of its Flora and Environment*, 1978

Carmichael, A. *Carmina Gadelica*, vols I-VI, Edinburgh 1928-71

Clancy, T.O. 'Iona, Scotland and the Céli Dé', in *Scotland in Dark Age Britain*, ed.Barbara E. Crawford (Scottish Cultural Press, 1996), Chapter 6, pp 111-130.

Clancy, T. O. and Márkus, G. *Iona. The Earliest Poetry of a Celtic Monastery*, Edinburgh 1995

Cumming, C.F.G. *From the Hebrides to the Himalayas*, 2nd edn London 1883

Faithfull, J. *The Ross of Mull Granite Quarries*, Iona 1995

Ferguson, M. *A Visit to Staffa and Iona*, Dundee & Edinburgh 1894

Ferguson, R. *George MacLeod*, London 1990

Forman, M.B. *The Letters of John Keats*, Oxford 1952

Garnett, T. *Observations on a Tour through the Highlands and part of the Western Isles of Scotland*, 2 vols, London 1810

Graham, H.D. *Antiquities of Iona*, London 1850

Graham, *The Birds of Iona and Mull 1852-1870*, Edinburgh 1890

Head, Sir G. *A Home Tour through various parts of the United Kingdom*, London 1837

Johnson, Dr. S. *A Journey to the Western Islands of Scotland (1773)*, London 1775

Johnson, J.(pseudonym Frederick Fag) *Recess in the Highlands and Lowlands*, London 1834

Keddie, W. *Staffa and Iona Described and Illustrated*, Glasgow 1850

Lumsden & Son's Steam-Boat Companion, 1st edn, Glasgow 1820

MacArthur, E.M. *Iona. The Living Memory of a Crofting Community 1750-1914*, Edinburgh 1990

MacArthur, E.M. *Columba's Island. Iona from Past to Present*, Edinburgh 1995

MacArthur, E.M. 'The Wreck of the *Guy Mannering*' in *Scottish World*, Feb/Mar 1992, p. 29

MacCormick, I. *The Celtic Art of Iona*, Iona 1994

MacCulloch, Dr. J., *The Highlands and Western Isles of Scotland*, 4 vols, London   1824

MacDonald, Revd C.A., 'The last New Year's Day Shinty Match in Iona', from personal correspondence, published in *Shinty Year Book*, 1991-92

MacFarlane's Geographical Collection, Vol. II, Scottish History Society, Edinburgh, Vol. LII, 1907

Martin, M. *A Description of the Western Islands of Scotland*, 1st edn, London 1703

Millar, J.M. *Flowers of Iona*, new edn, Iona 1993

Murray, The Hon. Mrs. S., *A Companion and Useful Guide to the Beauties in the West Highlands of Scotland and in the Hebrides*, Vol.II, London 1803

Pennant, T. *A Tour in Scotland and Voyage to the Hebrides 1772*, London 1776

Reeves, W., *Adamnani Vitae Sancti Columbae*, Dublin 1857

Richmond, J.C. *A Visit to Iona by an American Clergyman*, Glasgow 1849

Ritchie, A. and E., *Iona Past and Present with Maps*, 3rd edn Edinburgh 1934

Royal Commission on the Ancient and Historical Monuments of Scotland *Argyll. An Inventory of the Monuments, vol. 4 Iona*, Edinburgh 1982

Sacheverell, Dr. W. *An Account of the Isle of Man…with a Voyage to I-Columb-Kill*, London 1701

Sharpe, R. *Adomnán of Iona. Life of St Columba*, London 1995

Viner, D. *The Iona Marble Quarry*, new edn Iona 1992

Walker, Revd Dr J., *Report on the Hebrides of 1764 and 1771*, edited by M. M. McKay, Edinburgh 1980

MANUSCRIPT SOURCES :

Bute, J. 1st Marquess 'Journal of the Tour round the Western Islands of Scotland 1788', ms. 9587, National Library of Scotland

Douglas, W. 'Map of Iona, drawn 1769', Argyll Estate Papers

Lamont, A., 'Description of the Island of Iona or Icolmkill', ms written in 1848, typed copy in private hands

Ramsay of Ochtertyre, 18th century description of Beltane fire festival, ms. 1644, National Library of Scotland

Sibbald's Collection, 'A short description of I or Iona 1693', ms in private hands

ORAL SOURCES :

Sound Archive, School of Scottish Studies, University of Edinburgh, recordings made by author 1984-86; also author's own records.

Index